THE BOOK OF KISSES

ALSO BY WILLIAM CANE

The Art of Kissing

THE
ℬook
OF
𝒦ISSES

EDITED BY
WILLIAM CANE

ST. MARTIN'S PRESS
NEW YORK

For Judy Youngson, with love

THE BOOK OF KISSES. Copyright © 1993 by William Cane. All rights reserved.
Printed in the United States of America. No part of this book may be used
or reproduced in any manner whatsoever without written permission
except in the case of brief quotations embodied in critical
articles or reviews. For information, address St. Martin's Press,
175 Fifth Avenue, New York, N.Y. 10010.

Production Editor: David Stanford Burr

Design by Jaye Zimet

Library of Congress Cataloging-in-Publication Data

The Book of kisses : a definitive collection of the most passionate,
romantic, outlandish, and wonderful quotations on the intimate art
of kissing / [edited by] William Cane.
p.   cm.
ISBN 0-312-08710-1 (pbk.)
1. Kissing—Quotations, maxims, etc. I. Cane, William.
PN6084.K5B66   1993
394—dc20   92-39748   CIP

First Edition: February 1993

10   9   8   7   6   5   4   3   2   1

CONTENTS

PREFACE

*K*iss! Kiss! Kiss! Kiss!
Smack! Smack! Smmmmmmack!
It's back in style and more popular than ever!
Just read their lips!

A recent survey of about five thousand readers of *True Romance* and other such magazines found that 68 percent of women preferred kissing and cuddling to making love. Incredible! But good news for all who love kissing and petting sessions that go on into the wee hours. What can you say in response to a survey like that . . . except maybe "Take me to your parlor!"

Is kissing really so popular?

Those crazy statistics! The majority of women surveyed prefer kissing to any other sexual acts. They prefer it! They would rather be kissing!

Ever since I wrote *The Art of Kissing* (St. Martin's Press, 1991), I've been giving lectures on the subject at colleges, and a group of undergraduates always eagerly volunteer to stand up on the stage to demonstrate the kisses I'm discussing. These students love to kiss! The audience gets a big kick out of this, and usually laughs nonstop for about an hour. I start talking about the biting kiss, and my volunteers start biting each other's earlobes. I talk about the French kiss and their tongues go to work. I describe the electric kiss and they rub their feet on the rug (we always have a rug to demonstrate this one), shocking each other with static electricity when they kiss.

Recently I spoke at Bentley College to a group of undergraduates who laughed when I told them about kissing while talking. They thought that was very funny. But most people do break off from a kiss now and then to say something to their partner. It's so easy. You just move your mouth up to your partner's ear and whisper something romantic . . .

"Where're the mints?"

If you've ever been at a loss for words in that kind of situation, this book of quotations will give you plenty of ideas. Say something funny with a quote from the chapter on humorous kisses. Say something sweet with a line from the chapter on romantic kisses. Say something that will lead in a new direction with a quote from the kissing technique chapter. Or raise the stakes with a quote from the chapter on sensual kisses.

Need I even suggest that you can also use these quotes as a prelude to kissing? On a winter night, open the book at fireside and read to your lover at random from any page. Soon the book will be on the floor, your lover will be in your arms, the quotes will be swirling about in your head like snowflakes, and your kisses will be making the room warm with love.

Finally, don't be surprised if some of these quotes inspire you to try new types of kisses. The technique chapter is best for that purpose, but many of the other chapters will also introduce you to new kisses. If you need more advanced coaching I suggest you do whatever you can to get your hands on a copy of *The Art of Kissing*.

While there isn't space to mention everyone who helped me

with this manuscript, I would like to thank Carla Mayer Glasser for giving me the idea for the book in the first place.

Yes, it's back in style! And *The Book of Kisses* will help you kiss, and talk about kissing, with the kind of world-knowing flair that will have your lovers saying "Where did you hear that, dear?" Ah, *The Book of Kisses*! From their lips to yours . . .

❤

THE BOOK OF KISSES

HOW THEY KISS

What man hasn't wondered what it would be like to kiss Kim Basinger or Madonna? What woman hasn't wondered what it would be like to kiss Woody Allen or Kevin Costner? In the following quotes you'll find out just how these and other celebrities kiss.

♥

DONALD TRUMP

He's a wonderful kisser.

KIM ALLEY, MODEL

MADONNA

I was terrified. I'd never kissed anybody on screen, and I came clean with her. I said, "I'm like kind of new at this." And she was really nice about it. In fact she was really nice the whole time. She taught me how to do the kissing, and then she joked, "If you slip me the tongue, I'll kill you."

MICHAEL MEYERS OF *WAYNE'S WORLD*; *SATURDAY NIGHT LIVE* COMEDIAN

KEVIN COSTNER

Kissing him was just fine. We didn't practice. There was divine intervention and we just clicked.

MARY ELIZABETH MASTRANTONIO

He's a very good kisser . . . Those kinds of scenes, you can't help but feel vulnerable.

MARY McDONNELL, ACTOR

MICKEY ROURKE

Kissing Mickey is like kissing an ashtray.

KIM BASINGER

KIM BASINGER

When I read the part in the script where my character kisses Kim, I started screaming, "I get to kiss Kim Basinger? I get to kiss her? Of course I'll do it. I don't need to read the rest of the script!"

JON LOVITZ, ACTOR IN THE FILM *MY STEPMOTHER IS AN ALIEN*

Getting to kiss Kim Basinger wasn't too bad. And I didn't get the kiss right the first time, either. My mama didn't raise a fool. I wasn't going to get it right, come on! After take 20, or 25, I was saying, "Yeah, I'm starting to get the motivation now."

ROBERT WUHL, COMEDIAN (DISCUSSING KISSING ON THE SET OF *BATMAN*)

LEONARD BERNSTEIN

When Lenny would greet you, he'd throw his arms around you and kiss you on the mouth. Some of us didn't want it—but that's the way he was. Even his excess was real. It wasn't something he added as an afterthought.

ROBERT SHAW, CONDUCTOR

GEORGE BUSH

I put my hand out to shake hands out of respect. He leaned over for a kiss . . . He was sweet.

BROOKE SHIELDS

LARRY KING

His kiss was wet.

DYAN CANNON

RICHARD BURTON

Burton kissed with all the passion of a Roman statue and not just because he was usually stoned.

MICHAEL KILIAN, *THE CHICAGO TRIBUNE*

ARNOLD SCHWARZENEGGER

I taught him how to kiss, and he taught me how to take the punch in the movie—that was my first stunt.

PENELOPE ANN MILLER (DISCUSSING KISSING ARNOLD SCHWARZENEGGER IN

KINDERGARTEN COP)

BONNIE RAITT

She's so nice, so good—and so sexy. The other day I hadn't seen her for quite a while, and she kissed me on the lips. Just a little kiss, but it was very, very knowing.

BRUCE SPRINGSTEEN

ORSON WELLES

Orson Welles kissed me with his soul, never with his lips.

EARTHA KITT

GRETA GARBO

She kissed as thirstily as ever, cupping her man's head in both hands and seeming very nearly to drink from it.

KENNETH TYNAN

DUSTIN HOFFMAN

Dustin was great, by the way, just great. And yes, I kissed him in *Tootsie* and he's a very good kisser.

CHARLES DURNING

CLARK GABLE

Clark Gable I remember being a very nice "daddy." His mustache scratched when he kissed me.

CAMMIE KING CONLON, WHO PLAYED RHETT AND SCARLETT'S FOUR-YEAR-OLD
DAUGHTER IN *GONE WITH THE WIND*

PAUL NEWMAN

I did the scene and it's just two words. But, let me tell you, when you can sit at a table and Paul Newman makes an entrance and *kisses you on the naked shoulder,* and then you look up in those eyes and say, very casually, "Hello, Governor," that's acting. For a woman, *that* is acting.

BLAZE STARR

TELLY SAVALAS

Telly has such a sensuality to him, that quiet brewing. He looks like he's thinking of you in bed. Damn, the director cut before we could kiss.

ANGIE DICKINSON

LIBERACE

I had the pleasure of meeting him once. He actually kissed my hand. It was at a concert. He reached over the lady in front of me and said, "I don't know what you've been doing, baby, but keep up the good work."

DOLORES LANCASTER SCHMID, A FAN OF LIBERACE

ELVIS PRESLEY

I kissed Elvis every night from the second date on. He was a good kisser. But the nuns at my school told us we shouldn't allow boys to kiss us with their mouths open. So I'll just say Elvis gave me long kisses on prom night. You could say we made out. But he never tried to go farther. He wasn't like that.

REGIS WILSON VAUGHN, ELVIS'S DATE AT THE 1953 PROM AT L. C. HUMES HIGH SCHOOL IN MEMPHIS, TENNESSEE

RAQUEL WELCH

I kissed Raquel's ear, and her body jumped. Hmmmmm. I stuck my tongue in softly. Raquel started heating up, so did the scene . . . We took another break [and Raquel] said, "Jim, if you don't mind, please don't stick your tongue in my ear . . . It'll mess up my makeup."

JIM BROWN, FOOTBALL PLAYER TURNED MOVIE STAR

ALI MACGRAW

When Ali gave me this deep kiss [in *Love Story*] I knew she liked me. Then my friend saw the test and I said, "How about that kiss?" He said, "Hey, she kissed every guy like that." I was very disappointed.

RYAN O'NEAL

CARY GRANT

An elegant gray paisley robe covered most of him, but I could see part of his chest. God, he was attractive! . . . He reached over and kissed me gently. Then he put his arms around me, and the tenderness with which he surrounded me excited and moved me . . . Our bodies joined together and I could not believe the joy I felt.

MAUREEN DONALDSON, *AN AFFAIR TO REMEMBER*

WOODY ALLEN

Right before we shot that scene, Woody said to me, "I'm going to give you only one lip when we kiss. Because if I give you two, you'll never live through it." So I was laughing, because we were a little nervous. Those kisses were very sweet, as I recall.

ANDREA MARCOVICCI

MARLON BRANDO

He was so giving and considerate. Here it was my first scene in a movie, ever, and I have to lean over and kiss Marlon Brando. But he was so sweet, after a couple of days I felt like one of the gang . . . Oh, he was so attractive. I was so glad I was married at the time—newly married, but married—because he had it all.

EVA MARIE SAINT

PEE-WEE HERMAN (A. K. A. PAUL REUBENS)

He looks like he'd be fun to kiss. He's got nice lips.

PENELOPE ANN MILLER

ROBERT DE NIRO

He put his thumb in my mouth all the way, and then he pulled it all the way out. I'll tell you exactly what it felt like, emotionally—like someone walked up, penetrated you, and then walked away.

JULIETTE LEWIS (DISCUSSING HER KISSING SCENE WITH ROBERT DE NIRO IN *CAPE FEAR*)

ELIZABETH TAYLOR

The first time I met her on the set of *The VIPs,* I was pinching myself, she was so beautiful. She came up and kissed me and put a glass of champagne in my hand. It was about ten o'clock in the morning, and she looked as if twenty-five hairdressers had done her hair. She had on this beautiful nightdress. Big cleavage and all that. I deliberately looked at her eyes, for her not to think I was being rude.

GRAHAM JENKINS, YOUNGER BROTHER OF RICHARD BURTON

♥

FIRST KISSES

*I*f you've kissed your first kiss already, you might be tempted to skip over this chapter. But don't do it! Remember, there's always the first kiss with—someone new . . . and in the following quotes you may find exactly the kind of advice, encouragement, and humor that will help you accomplish your next first kiss.

❤

I remember the first time we admitted that we loved each other. It was in our second year, on the upstairs gallery that formed the entrance foyer to the Institute's assembly hall. And we kissed behind the pillars.

BORIS YELTSIN, ON KISSING NAYA YELTSIN

❤

We sat and kissed and kissed until our lips were bloody. I could have gone on kissing her for a year.

RYAN O'NEAL, ON HIS FIRST DATE WITH WIFE-TO-BE FARRAH FAWCETT

❤

So sweet love seemed that April morn,
When first we kissed beside the thorn,
So strangely sweet, it was not strange
We thought that love could never change.

ROBERT BRIDGES (1844–1930)

She lifted her delicate, high-bred face, fearless love shining in every lineament, to his, and they exchanged their first kiss.

LUCY MAUD MONTGOMERY, *BETWEEN THE HILL AND THE VALLEY*

I kissed my first girlfriend behind a Ben Franklin store.

DALE D. WARD, EXECUTIVE OF BEN FRANKLIN STORES

My first kiss can be summed up in one word: unsuccessful.

HUEY LEWIS, OF HUEY LEWIS AND THE NEWS

I think he [composer Joe Raposo] was the first man who kissed me on the cheek.

WALTER CRONKITE

My dear Mary, You struck the right thing about those kisses. There is not much in them on paper, but they are all right when they are real, by Jove, I know, don't you? I should think you would.

ERROL FLYNN (IN A LOVE LETTER TO MARY WHITE, HIS FIRST GIRLFRIEND)

It was really funny the way it happened. We were sitting on opposite sides of the room for about six hours going, "Well, I think we could hug." And we'd meet in the middle of the room, hug and go back. Then we'd go, "Okay, well maybe now we should kiss." So then we'd kiss and run back.

ROSEANNE BARR, ON KISSING TOM ARNOLD

Rosey [Roseanne Barr] and I didn't even kiss until she decided her marriage was over. We had been falling in love all those years, but we denied it to ourselves and everyone else. We never acted on our feelings because we didn't want to lose each other over a stupid thing we would later regret.

TOM ARNOLD

Only he felt he could no more dissemble,
And kissed her, mouth to mouth, all in a tremble.

LEIGH HUNT (1784–1859), *STORY OF RIMINI*

I was seventeen and the star of my high school play. I was supposed to kiss my leading man, but I couldn't stand the guy. I *really* didn't want to kiss him. All during rehearsals, I refused to kiss him. Then my drama teacher told me, "If you don't kiss him on opening night, you'll flunk drama class." So I kissed him, and that was my first kiss.

DONNA MILLS, WHO PLAYS ABBY EWING ON *KNOTS LANDING*

I was like twelve or something, when you first kiss a guy and you see the way the guy reacts, how they get really excited, or whatever. And I'm perceptive, so I think, "Ah, jeez, is that something that I'm able to do?"

JULIETTE LEWIS

I got into show business because I had never gotten kissed before and I wanted this boy to kiss me. I didn't know how you did it, and I wanted to do it right. The first rehearsal was such a failure that the teacher said, "That's okay, Polly, we'll do it later." It was pathetic.

POLLY DRAPER, WHO PLAYS ELLYN WARREN ON *THIRTYSOMETHING*

First time he kissed me, he but only kissed
The fingers of this hand wherewith I write;
And, ever since, it grew more clean and white.

ELIZABETH BARRETT BROWNING (1806–1861), *SONNETS FROM THE PORTUGUESE*, NUMBER 38

The decision to kiss for the first time is the most crucial in any love story. It changes the relationship of two people much more strongly than even the final surrender; because this kiss already has within it that surrender.

EMIL LUDWIG (1861–1948), *OF LIFE AND LOVE*

How delicious is the winning
Of a kiss at Love's beginning.

THOMAS CAMPBELL (1777–1844), *SONG*

Miss Manners herself, while never rude, is given to pulling a fast punch in the way of a handshake on those who believe in kissing on, not even the first date, but the first sighting.

JUDITH MARTIN (MISS MANNERS)

When age chills the blood, when our pleasures are past—
   For years fleet away with the wings of the dove—
The dearest remembrance will still be the last,
   Our sweetest memorial the first kiss of love.

LORD BYRON (1788–1824), *THE FIRST KISS OF LOVE*

Platonic friendship is the interval between the introduction and the first kiss.

R. WOODS, ED., *MODERN HANDBOOK OF HUMOR*

My lips till then had only known
   The kiss of mother and of sister,
But somehow, full upon her own
   Sweet, rosy, darling mouth,—I kissed her.

E. C. STEDMAN (1833–1908), *THE DOOR-STEP*

I kissed my first woman and smoked my first cigarette on the same day. I have never had time for tobacco since.

ARTURO TOSCANINI

KISSING DEFINED

*A*rtfully crafted, the very definition of the word *kiss* can inspire kissing. Which is why we have turned mostly to poets and other writers for the definitions that follow.

The dictionary says that a kiss is "a salute made by touching with the lips pressed closely together and suddenly parting them." From this it is quite obvious that, although a dictionary may know something about words, it knows nothing about kissing.

HUGH MORRIS, *THE ART OF KISSING* (1936)

A kiss can be a comma, a question mark, or an exclamation point. That's basic spelling that every woman ought to know.

MISTINGUETTE (JEANNE MARIE BOURGEOIS, FRENCH ACTOR), *THEATRE ARTS*,
December 1955

A kiss is strange. It's a living thing, a communication, a whole wild emotion expressed in a simple moist touch.

MICKEY SPILLANE, *THE KILLING MAN*

"Kiss" rhymes to "bliss" in fact as well as verse.
LORD BYRON (1788—1824), *DON JUAN*

♥

A word invented by the poets as a rhyme for "bliss."
AMBROSE BIERCE (1842—1914), *THE DEVIL'S DICTIONARY*

♥

Something made of nothing, tasting very sweet,
A most delicious compound, with ingredients complete;
But if, as on occasion, the heart and mind are sour,
It has no great significance, and loses half its power.
MARY E. BUELL (FLOURISHED AROUND 1890),
AMERICAN VERSE WRITER, *THE KISS*

♥

Kisses are like grains of gold or silver found upon the ground, of
no value themselves, but precious as showing that a mine is near.
GEORGE VILLIERS (1628—1687)

♥

The anatomical juxtaposition of two *orbicularis oris* muscles in a
state of contraction.
DR. HENRY GIBBONS, SR. (1808—1884)

♥

What is a kiss? Why this, as some approve:
The sure sweet cement, glue, and lime of love.
ROBERT HERRICK (1591—1674), *HESPERIDES*

♥

What is a kiss? Alacke! at worst,
A single Dropp to quenche a Thirst,
Tho' oft it prooves, in happie Hour,
The first sweet Dropp of our long Showre.

CHARLES GODFREY LELAND (1824–1903), *IN THE OLD TIME*

'Tis a secret
Told to the mouth instead of to the ear.

EDMOND ROSTAND (1868–1918), *CYRANO DE BERGERAC*

To a woman the first kiss is the end of the beginning; to a man
it is the beginning of the end.

HELEN ROWLAND (1876–1950)

Unspoken promise of a soul's allegiance.

MARION PHELPS

A thing of use to no one, but prized by two.

ROBERT ZWICKEY

That which you cannot give without taking, and cannot take
without giving.

ANONYMOUS

A contraction of the mouth due to an enlargement of the heart.

ANONYMOUS

A kiss is a lovely trick designed by nature to stop speech when words become superfluous.

INGRID BERGMAN

A vigorous exchange of saliva.

CAPTAIN VAN VELSOR, PHYSICAL EDUCATOR,
RENSSELAER POLYTECHNIC INSTITUTE

Lip service to love.

WARREN GOLDBERG

Kisses are like confidences—one follows the other.

DENIS DIDEROT (1713–1784)

A kiss is now attestedly a quite innocuous performance, with nothing very fearful about it one way or the other. It even has a pleasant side.

JAMES BRANCH CABELL, *JURGEN* (1919)

Traditional Hollywood-style greeting for friend and foe alike.

EUGENE E. BRUSSELL

Something that often leads to marriage because it leaves something to be desired.

ADAPTED FROM ROBERT FONTAINE

When soul meets soul on lovers' lips.
PERCY BYSSHE SHELLEY (1792–1822), *PROMETHEUS UNBOUND*

A kiss is like singing into someone's mouth.
DIANE ACKERMAN, *A NATURAL HISTORY OF THE SENSES*

A pleasant reminder that two heads are better than one.
REX PROUTY

A kiss is a noun both common and proper,
Not very singular; and agrees with both *you* and *me*.
ANONYMOUS

MOVIE AND TV KISSES

*A*ccording to a 1992 Gallup poll, Americans believe the sexiest movie kiss is the one between Rhett Butler and Scarlett O'Hara in *Gone With the Wind*. Next most memorable is the one between Burt Lancaster and Deborah Kerr in *From Here to Eternity*. Third is the one in *Casablanca* between Humphrey Bogart and Ingrid Bergman.

While not all movie kisses are passionate, you might be surprised at how glamorous and knowing you'll appear to your date when you break off from a kiss and recite one or two lines from a movie. Also included here are quotes about movies and from directors for an inside look at how screen kisses are conceived and executed. Actors talk about kissing beginning on page 33.

♥

"I want you to faint. That's what you were meant for. None of the fools you've ever known have kissed you like this, have they?"

CLARK GABLE TO VIVIEN LEIGH IN *GONE WITH THE WIND* (MGM, 1939)

♥

"Hey, listen, listen, give me a kiss?"

"Really?"

"Yeah, why not? Because we're just going to go home later, right? And there's going to be all that tension, you know, we never kissed before, and I'll never know when to make the right move or anything. So we'll kiss now and get it over with, and then we'll go eat. Okay? We'll digest our food better."

WOODY ALLEN AND DIANE KEATON IN *ANNIE HALL* (UNITED ARTISTS, 1977)

"I have so many kisses and so many hugs. I have a trillion jillion of them."

CHRISTINE LAHTI IN *FUNNY ABOUT LOVE* (PARAMOUNT, 1990)

Man in bar: What would I have to give you for a little kiss?

Woman: Chloroform.

FOR THE BOYS (20TH CENTURY–FOX, 1991)

"I know how you feel. You don't know whether you want to hit me or kiss me. I get a lot of that."

MADONNA TO WARREN BEATTY IN *DICK TRACY*

(TOUCHSTONE/SILVER SCREEN PARTNERS IV, 1990)

"I got a funny sensation in my toes. Like someone was barbecuing them over a slow flame."

"Let's throw another log on the fire."

MARILYN MONROE AND TONY CURTIS IN *SOME LIKE IT HOT*

(ASHTON/MIRISCH, 1959)

"I believe in long, slow, deep, soft, wet kisses that last for three days."

KEVIN COSTNER IN *BULL DURHAM* (MOUNT/ORION, 1988)

"Come here, ya lug!"
"Well, it's about time."

CLARK GABLE AND JEAN HARLOW IN *RED DUST* (MGM, 1932)

"Here's a soldier of the South who loves you, Scarlett, wants to feel your arms around him, wants to carry the memory of your kisses into battle with him. Never mind about loving me. You're a woman, sending a soldier to his death with a beautiful memory. Scarlett, kiss me. Kiss me, once."

CLARK GABLE TO VIVIEN LEIGH IN *GONE WITH THE WIND* (MGM, 1939)

"I don't know how to kiss, or I would kiss you. Where do the noses go?"

INGRID BERGMAN TO GARY COOPER IN *FOR WHOM THE BELL TOLLS*

(PARAMOUNT, 1943)

"I don't know why I should act so experienced. It was only my second kiss this year."

DIANE VARSI TO RUSS TAMBLYN IN *PEYTON PLACE* (20TH CENTURY-FOX, 1957)

"It's even better when you help."

LAUREN BACALL TO HUMPHREY BOGART IN *TO HAVE AND HAVE NOT*

(WARNER BROS., 1944)

"When a woman kisses me, Louise, she has to take pot luck."
_{VAN HEFLIN TO JOAN CRAWFORD IN *POSSESSED* (WARNER BROS., 1947)}

♥

"Where did you learn to kiss like that?"
"I used to sell kisses for the milk fund."
"Tomorrow, remind me to send a check for $100,000 to the milk fund."

_{TONY CURTIS (FIRST SPEAKER) TO MARILYN MONROE IN *SOME LIKE IT HOT*}

_(UNITED ARTISTS, 1959)

♥

"Please just kiss me once."
"If I kissed you once, you wouldn't ask anymore?"
"Just once."
"On the lips or mouth?"
"Mouth."
"I only kiss Mrs. Hillyer on the mouth."

_{LAURA DERN (FIRST SPEAKER) AND ROBERT DUVALL AS SHE JUMPS ONTO HIS LAP,}

_{BEGGING AND RECEIVING A KISS IN *RAMBLING ROSE* (NEW LINE, 1991)}

♥

"All right* . . . all right* . . . all right.*"
"Get out of here."
"I got to go."
"Bye."
"All right* . . . I'm not leaving here."
"Get out of here."
"All right. Later."
"Later."*

_{SPIKE LEE (FIRST SPEAKER) AND ROSIE PEREZ IN *DO THE RIGHT THING* IN A LOVE}

_{SCENE WHERE THEIR LIPS FILL THE ENTIRE SCREEN. THE ASTERISKS INDICATE}

_{EACH TIME THEY KISS. (40 ACRES & A MULE, 1989)}

"You are very talkative."

"Was that talkative?"

"No, that was restful. Again."

GRETA GARBO (FIRST SPEAKER) TO MELVYN DOUGLAS IN *NINOTCHKA*.
HE KISSES HER AFTER THE FIRST LINE. (MGM 1939)

"Why do I get the feeling that if I reach out and touch you you'll disappear?"

"Why don't you try it and see?"

CARRÉ OTIS (FIRST SPEAKER) AND MICKEY ROURKE BEFORE SHE EMBRACES HIM
AND KISSES HIM ON THE NECK IN *WILD ORCHID* (VISION, 1990)

"I ain't a rich man. You could get a rich man if you tried."

"I don't want no rich man!"

"You ain't gonna have a minute's peace."

"You promise?"

WARREN BEATTY (FIRST SPEAKER) AND FAYE DUNAWAY IN *BONNIE & CLYDE*
BEFORE CLYDE KISSES HER ON THE BED IN THEIR HIDEOUT
(WARNER/SEVEN ARTS/TATIRA-HILLER, 1967)

"Say 'kiss me.' "

"Kiss me."

" 'I want you.' "

"I want you."

"Again."

"I want you. Put your hands on me."

HARRISON FORD (FIRST SPEAKER) EXCHANGES A KISS WITH AN ANDROID PLAYED
BY SEAN YOUNG, GIVING HER A LESSON IN HUMAN LOVE IN
BLADE RUNNER (WARNER/LADD, 1982)

"I will not have my face smeared with lipstick. If you want to kiss me, kiss me on the lips, which is what a merciful providence provided them for."

HERBERT MARSHALL TO GENE TIERNEY IN *THE RAZOR'S EDGE*
(20TH CENTURY—FOX, 1946)

"When a clumsy cloud from here meets a fluffy little cloud from there, he billows towards her. She scurries away, and he scuds right up to her. She cries a little, and there you have your shower. He comforts her. They spark. That's the lightning. They kiss. Thunder!"

FRED ASTAIRE TO GINGER ROGERS IN *TOP HAT* (RKO RADIO, 1935)

"William, that was *not* a preacher's kiss!"

SUSAN HAYWARD TO WILLIAM LUNDIGAN IN *I'D RATHER CLIMB THE HIGHEST
MOUNTAIN* (20TH CENTURY—FOX, 1951)

"I have a message for your wife. Don't wipe it off. If she thinks that's cranberry sauce, tell her she's got cherry pits in her head."

MARILYN MONROE TO TOM EWELL IN *THE SEVEN YEAR ITCH*
(20TH CENTURY—FOX, 1955)

"I'd love to kiss you but I just washed my hair."

BETTE DAVIS IN *CABIN IN THE COTTON* (WARNER BROS., 1932)

"And from this slumber you shall wake
When true love's kiss the spell shall break."

MAGICAL FAIRY TO SLEEPING BEAUTY IN *SLEEPING BEAUTY*
(WALT DISNEY, 1959)

"It's going to be okay . . . okay . . . okay . . . I'll make some tea."
"Harry, could you just hold me a little longer?"
"Oh, sure."

BILLY CRYSTAL COMFORTING MEG RYAN, WHO IS CRYING BEFORE THEY HAVE
THEIR FIRST ROMANTIC KISS IN *WHEN HARRY MET SALLY*
(CASTLE ROCK/NELSON/COLUMBIA, 1989)

❤

She: What do you want?
He: What do you do?
She: Everything. But I don't kiss on the mouth.
He: Neither do I.

RICHARD GERE AND JULIA ROBERTS, WHO PLAYS A PROSTITUTE, IN
PRETTY WOMAN (TOUCHSTONE, 1990)

❤

"I love you so much. That's the one thing I never said to you
because I was afraid of losing you forever."

RAUL JULIA TO HIS LOVER BEFORE HE KISSES HER IN A MORPHINE-INDUCED
DREAM IN *KISS OF THE SPIDER WOMAN* (SUGARLOAF/HB FILMES, 1985)

❤

"I was born when you kissed me. I died when you left me. I lived
a few days while you loved me."

HUMPHREY BOGART TO GLORIA GRAHAME IN *IN A LONELY PLACE*
(COLUMBIA, 1950)

❤

"Frankly, my child, I had a sudden, powerful, and very ignoble
desire to kiss you till your lips were somewhat bruised."

DAVID NIVEN TO MAGGIE MCNAMARA IN *THE MOON IS BLUE*
(UNITED ARTISTS, 1953)

ALL ABOUT MOVIE KISSING

Kissing . . . in the old days was very beautiful. Actually the two people doing it were barely touching sometimes, in order to not push her face out of shape. You were doing it for the audience to see what in their minds they always think a kiss is. Now you see a couple of people start chewing on each other.

RONALD REAGAN (ON HOLLYWOOD KISSING STYLES),

NBC TV, MARCH 24, 1986

Some kisses are about sealing a deal—the one Gable gives Vivien Leigh after he proposes to her in *Gone With the Wind*. It's not about love. It's negotiation because he understands she's marrying him for his money . . . Spencer Tracy and Katharine Hepburn provided equality kisses in all their movies. They were peers, almost like shaking hands. They weren't passionate.

LENA TABORI

These days movie kissing is merely a necessary stop on the road to the graphic depiction of more intimate contact.

RICK KOGAN, TV/RADIO CRITIC, *CHICAGO TRIBUNE*

That's why they have the so-called sex films. When you see a boy and a girl kissing now, they kiss until someone in the audience has an orgasm. They just don't kiss and let it go at that. They want the audience to have an orgasm, so they'll come back again.

WALTER MATTHAU

DIRECTOR'S KISSES

I studied very carefully the best way to photograph a kiss, but Mel [Gibson] was very nervous. We rehearsed where they first kissed [in the movie *The Year of Living Dangerously*]. Mel took Sigourney [Weaver] outside an embassy party, pushed her against a wall and kissed her, but it didn't work. I took Mel aside and asked, "What's wrong?" He said, "I'm kissing fine. Talk to Sigourney." She said, "Talk to Mel." Finally I thought, The only way to know is to kiss Sigourney myself. I called a break and I said, "Someone is not pressing right." I asked Sigourney to kiss my hand. She thought that was so funny she told Mel, and by the time we got back from dinner the ice was broken. They had just been trying too hard.

PETER WEIR, AUSTRALIAN DIRECTOR

"I love women . . . But I didn't meet any girls until I was about nineteen. I remember kissing one of the maids once. And then you go slightly mad, raving mad, when you do find a woman.

DAVID LEAN, FILM DIRECTOR

In the whole closing sequence at Casablanca Airport, there's no kiss. Think about it, probably the most romantic movie ever, and it doesn't end with a kiss.

BRUCE COHEN, DIRECTOR AND PRODUCER OF THE CABLE TV SHOW *KISSES*

Growing up, I never saw black people kiss on film, never saw black sexuality, because Hollywood was afraid to show that. We kiss and make love like anybody else. Why shouldn't black people make love on screen?

SPIKE LEE

❤

ADVICE ABOUT KISSES

When it comes to dispensing free advice about kissing it seems that everybody has something to say. Most of these quotes contain good suggestions, but be forewarned: some are humorous or just plain ridiculous. If you can figure out which is which, you'll have at your disposal the kind of advice that can make your kissing easier, happier, sexier, more thrilling, and generally more pleasing to both you and your lover. But perhaps the only way you'll know if they work is to try them and see.

My child, if you finally decide to let a man kiss you, put your whole heart and soul into it. No man likes to kiss a rock.

LADY CHESTERFIELD

If you are ever in doubt as to whether or not you should kiss a pretty girl, always give her the benefit of the doubt.

THOMAS CARLYLE (1795–1881)

Why don't you kiss your man unexpectedly every chance you have? Get him used to being bussed in public.

COSMOPOLITAN

You don't know how to kiss and flirt unless you do it.

DEBORAH THURSTON

Don't wait to know her better to kiss her; kiss her, and you'll know her better.

ANONYMOUS

Always kiss your husband's body starting from his toes. After kissing his toes and sucking them, proceed to kiss every inch of his legs.

MELISSA SADOFF (ALSO KNOWN AS LADY STEVENS OF LUDGATE), *WOMAN AS CHAMELEON: HOW TO BE AN IDEAL WOMAN*

Teach not thy lip such scorn, for it was made
For kissing, lady, not for such contempt.

WILLIAM SHAKESPEARE, *RICHARD III*

Speak, cousin, or, if you cannot, stop his mouth with a kiss.

SHAKESPEARE, *MUCH ADO ABOUT NOTHING*

Lips go dry and eyes grow wet
Waiting to be warmly met.
Keep them not in waiting yet;
Kisses kept are wasted.

EDMUND VANCE COOKE, *KISSES KEPT ARE WASTED*

You must not kiss and tell.

WILLIAM CONGREVE (1670–1729), *LOVE FOR LOVE*

You should not take a fellow eight years old
And make him swear to never kiss the girls.

ROBERT BROWNING (1812–1861), *FRA LIPPO LIPPI*

Kiss her until she be wearied out.

SHELLEY (1792–1822), *TO NIGHT*

I say, when there are spats, kiss and make up before the day is
done and live to fight another day.

REV. RANDOLPH RAY, QUOTED IN THE *NEW YORK WORLD TELEGRAM*

JUNE 30, 1956

There are all sorts of kisses, lad, from the sticky confection to the kiss of death. Of them all, the kiss of an actress is the most unnerving. How can we tell if she means it or if she's just practicing?

RUTH GORDON (1896–1985), AMERICAN ACTOR, PLAYWRIGHT,
SCREENWRITER, *THE LEADING LADY*

Kiss the place to make it well.

ANN TAYLOR (1782–1866), *ORIGINAL POEMS FOR INFANT MINDS*,
"MY MOTHER"

Learn your lines. Don't bump into furniture. And in the kissing scenes, keep your mouth closed.

RONALD REAGAN, GIVING ADVICE TO SENATORS

WARNING ADVICE

When the girl you kiss gives as good as you give, you are not getting firsts.

ANONYMOUS

A kiss that speaks volumes is seldom a first edition.

OHIO STATE SUN DIAL

There is no more disturbing experience in the rich gamut of life than when a young man discovers, in the midst of an embrace, that he is taking the episode quite calmly, and is taking the kiss for what it is worth. His doubts and fears start from this point and there is no end to them. He doesn't know, now, whether it's love or passion. In fact, in the confusion of the moment he's not quite sure it isn't something else altogether, like forgery.

E. B. WHITE, *NEW YORK JOURNAL-AMERICAN*

❤

ACTOR KISSES

*W*hat a life! Kissing on the job and getting paid for it! They even have a chance to rehearse their kisses so that by the time their image is projected onto the silver screen they appear glamorous and godlike. Yet in the following quotes, you'll see just how down-to-earth and human these actors really are when it comes to kissing other actors.

I've not been comfortable with them [love scenes]. You think about them the night before. You don't want to be embarrassed. It's very difficult to get me to take off my shirt. I don't know why. I just feel awkward doing it. I've done it, but I just don't do it at the drop of a hat. I mean, I'm not a prude. You've seen my movies. I always depend on the script . . . Now everybody knows how I kiss.

KEVIN COSTNER

I get jealous whenever I watch Loni do a love scene. The worst is when Loni comes toward the actor like a grouper. Why is it necessary for her to open her mouth four feet from him? I've never understood why Americans think open-mouth kissing is sexy. I resent it when Loni does it, and that's why I can't watch it.

BURT REYNOLDS (ON WATCHING HIS WIFE, LONI ANDERSON)

There was a time when my older sisters and their friends were just starting to kiss boys. They needed somebody to practice on. I'd sprint home from school, go in the bathroom, and they'd put me on the bathroom sink, and my sister's two friends would take turns kissing me. They taught me how to French kiss when I was eight years old. The first time I almost suffocated.

TOM CRUISE

I don't want to sound like a prude because I'm not. But even in kissing scenes—like Tom Cruise and Kelly McGillis in *Top Gun*—who wants to see open mouths and tongues on a huge screen? Makes me want to take a shower.

GEORGE NEWBERN, TV AND MOVIE ACTOR

It depends on the people. I mean, are we discussing tongues vs. no tongues? . . . Let's see. I didn't tongue Chevy Chase in my new film, *Valkenvania,* but I did tongue Patrick Swayze [in *Ghost*] . . . I tongued Rob Lowe [*St. Elmo's Fire*], but before the videotape.

DEMI MOORE

I wouldn't pay money to see me kiss somebody.

JOHN CANDY

❤

My girlfriend always wants to know my every thought when I'm in these little love scenes. So I make up stuff. I tell her it has to be romantic, otherwise it looks soap-operaish. I tell her I'm kissing someone else but I'm thinking of her. I say, "I have to get into it for a bit, but only for a little while. Then I can come home and take it out on you."

BRIAN WIMMER, ACTOR IN *LATE FOR DINNER* AND *CHINA BEACH*

❤

We were home in bed watching that night, and Randy started yelling, "You're really kissing him!" I told him, "It's acting, honey."

SUSAN RUTTAN, ROXANNE MELMAN ON *L. A. LAW*

❤

When I watch a love scene today I just turn my eyes away. Especially those kissing scenes! My God, you can't tell whose tongue is in whose mouth!

LANA TURNER

❤

The boys let me know I was ugly. By sixteen or seventeen, there were some who thought I was attractive and would want to kiss me, but I was well into my twenties before anybody found me interesting.

LIV ULLMANN

❤

I was pretty crazed that day when I had to kiss Andy [Garcia] at seven in the morning. I wasn't feeling very romantic, and also the script supervisor, whom I've known since I was twelve, was standing a foot away saying, "OK, saliva under his left ear, Sofia." I mean, all this flirting and kissing I'm doing with Andy, I'm doing in front of my father, of all people!

SOFIA COPPOLA, DAUGHTER OF DIRECTOR FRANCIS FORD COPPOLA (TALKING
ABOUT HER ROLE IN *THE GODFATHER: PART III*)

❤

It took a very long while before I could portray the role the way they wanted me to, because I had to get the passion, the falling-in-love part, and that was very hard for me. Because I'd never fallen in love. And doing the kissing scenes . . . that was really a shock.

LEA SALONGA, AGE NINETEEN, ACTOR IN *MISS SAIGON*, A HIT MUSICAL IN
LONDON

❤

Deathtrap was a thriller about two gay murderers. We had to kiss each other in that film. We [Christopher Reeve and Caine] have a clause in our contracts in this one that we don't have to kiss.

MICHAEL CAINE

❤

The first time we did it I frantically sprayed Gold Spot in my mouth. Then I looked round and Annie [Kirkbride], who plays Deirdre, was doing exactly the same thing. It was absolutely hilarious. After that I decided to enjoy it.

DAVE BECKETT, A STAR OF *CORONATION STREET*

❤

Sidney Sheldon: Don't you want to do this scene?
Judy Garland: No. Because I have to kiss Fred [Astaire] in it and I've never met him.

❤

Actually, you're rarely naked, but you do get into some intimate positions, and, of course, you do kiss properly. My solution to the potential awkwardness is to joke about it a lot so that the actress I'm with is never under the impression that I'm getting off on it.

MICHAEL CAINE

❤

Kirk [Cameron] is always playing jokes on me. When we had our big kiss, he rubbed Anbesol on his mouth so when I kissed him, my mouth went numb.

CHELSEA NOBLE, WHO PLAYS KATE ON *GROWING PAINS*

❤

In second grade, I got sent to the principal for kissing a girl at recess.

RANDY QUAID

❤

I know it sounds weird, but I couldn't kiss someone knowing their saliva had impurities.

MARTHA PLIMPTON, TWENTY, A VEGETARIAN ACTOR

❤

The chemistry between Tim [Matheson] and me was wonderful, which you really need for a romantic comedy. We had to do a lot of kissing and after a while it became technical just figuring out how to do it different each time.

ANN JILLIAN, STAR OF THE NBC COMEDY SERIES OF THE SAME NAME

To start with, there were a couple of girls I kissed in a picture, but the kids wrote letters. We got letters from so many people. They thought it was sissy for me, a two-fisted cowboy, to go around kissing, so that was more or less eliminated.

GENE AUTRY

Whenever I have to kiss someone such as Jason Priestley, I usually introduce my boyfriend to the one I'm doing the love scene with. Then I have fun. I go for it.

GABRIELLE CARTERIS, WHO PLAYS ANDREA ZUCKERMAN

ON *BEVERLY HILLS 90210*

Suppose you are ready for the clinch. You face the girl and look down at her—if you aren't tall enough, you stand on a box. When the camera starts, the director tells you to take the girl in your arms and kiss her. That ought to be easy, but it isn't. The hairdresser stands by looking daggers at you if you muss the girl's hair. So you loop your arms around her neck, making sure you don't tilt her collar, and you look to your own appearance. Eventually you kiss the girl—only you can't kiss her square on the lips because if you do your nose hides her eyes. You kiss her just off center and she smacks into the air in response. Screen love is the bunk—but it's a living.

WAYNE MORRIS

I had to kiss a train window while looking through it at Woody [Allen] sitting at another train window. I was supposed to leave my lipstick mark on the glass. After I kissed the window, Woody came over and said, "I want you to do it again and do it like you're really kissing me." Next time I laid one on that window that steamed up the entire train.

SHARON STONE

ROMANTIC KISSES

*T*hese kisses are what you live for. They make you literally ache with pleasure. They light you up and send shocks through your nerves for hours and days afterward. They have you laughing and crying and doubting your sanity and wanting to stay up all night just so you can remember them. The magic that transforms these kisses is the stuff of romance. They are much more likely to occur in a romantic setting, under moonlight, on a beach, at fireside, or in a spot that has special meaning for both lovers. They may occur after years of separation or friendship, when feelings rise to the surface after prolonged denial or holding back, transforming an otherwise normal kiss into a special event, something tender, passionate, touching. These quotes hint at that feeling, but you've got to feel it to know what it's all about. And once you feel it, how can you ever forget?

❤

She went five stops past her stop 'cause she knew I was looking at her. When we got off the bus she gave me her number and a kiss on the cheek and—I'm serious—my heart was the size of a softball.

STEPHEN BALDWIN, STAR OF ABC's THE YOUNG RIDERS (ON MEETING HIS WIFE-TO-BE, KENNYA)

♥

I said, "He's too old, he has too many children and I'm not interested." . . . [Then] he kissed me on the back of my neck, and it sent this rush through me, and I went, "Oh, shoot."

MISSY THORNEBURG, WIFE OF MILLIONAIRE "BIG JIM" THORNEBURG

♥

A man had given all other bliss,
And all his worldly worth for this,
To waste his whole heart in one kiss
Upon her perfect lips.

LORD TENNYSON (1809–1892), SIR LAUNCELOT AND QUEEN GUINEVERE

♥

He was going to kiss her! She knew it, and yet she could not resist him as his lips touched her. She had never been kissed. Not even by Jasper. With an instinct as old as woman herself, Arabella's lips softened beneath his mouth. The kiss deepened, and she only realized it when she fell back upon her pillows, feeling the down give beneath her even as the passion suddenly ignited between them began to mount in its intensity.

BEATRICE SMALL, THE SPITFIRE

♥

You know, darling, that I love you too much to want to [kiss someone else]. If I did have an honest—or dishonest—desire to kiss just one or two people, I *might*—but I couldn't ever want to—my mouth is yours.

ZELDA SAYRE (IN A LETTER TO HER FUTURE HUSBAND, F. SCOTT FITZGERALD)

And when my lips meet thine,
Thy very soul is wedded unto mine.

H. H. BOYESEN (1848–1895), *THY GRACIOUS FACE
I GREET WITH GLAD SURPRISE*

When they kissed it seemed as if they did indeed imbibe each other, as if each were wine to the other's thirst.

ROBERT SPEAIGHT, *THE UNBROKEN HEART*

The song of songs, which is Solomon's.
Let him kiss me with the kisses of his mouth: for thy love is better than wine.

BIBLE, SONG OF SOLOMON 1:1-2

As he kissed her again, Lord Selwyn knew that he had found what all men seek. It is the love which is pure, perfect and undefiled, the love which comes from God, and is eternal.

BARBARA CARTLAND, *PARADISE IN PENANG*

Many an evening by the waters did we watch the stately ships,
And our spirits rush'd together at the touching of the lips.

TENNYSON (1809–1892), *LOCKSLEY HALL*

Wouldn't I like to kiss, hug, love, and almost devour you if I could only have you to myself today.

ALICE KIRK GRIERSON, WIFE OF CIVIL WAR OFFICER

♥

I love kissing. I love caressing. I love sex. In fact, I think sex is so great I can hardly wait. But I can wait because I know when I find a mate we'll be able to enjoy being physical for the rest of our lives together.

MARY MEYER, FOUNDER OF THE NATIONAL CHASTITY ASSOCIATION

♥

It was thy kiss, Love, that made me immortal.

MARGARET WITTER FULLER (1810–1850), AMERICAN POET, *DRYAD SONG*

♥

And our lips found ways of speaking
    What words cannot say,
Till a hundred nests gave music,
    And the East was gray.

FREDERICK LAWRENCE KNOWLES (1869–1905), AMERICAN POET, *A MEMORY*

♥

You must remember this, a kiss is still a kiss,
A sigh is just a sigh . . .

AS TIME GOES BY (1931 SONG)

♥

See the mountains kiss high Heaven
And the waves clasp one another;
No sister-flower would be forgiven
If it disdained its brother;
And the sunlight clasps the earth
And the moonbeams kiss the sea:
What are all these kissings worth
If thou kiss not me?

SHELLEY (1792—1822), *LOVE'S PHILOSOPHY*

CELEBRITY KISSES

*C*elebrities have said some pretty silly things about kissing, and some have said things worth noting. Assembled here is a collection of their more inspired utterances.

❤

I like to be kissed if I'm being screwed.
LEONA HELMSLEY

❤

Perhaps you're surprised by the fact that the Pope, even though he's a step away from the children, doesn't hug and kiss them. He was about to do so, but then he thought that he has a virus, and since there's enough influenza going around, there isn't reason to add more.

POPE JOHN PAUL II AT A ROME PARISH

❤

I was embarrassed. The whole world is going to watch me kiss. But I do like it.

DR. RUTH WESTHEIMER (COMMENTING ON HER KISS ON THE ABC-TV SERIES SHE WILL STAR IN)

❤

Carrie Fisher: Do they [women] kiss the same as men?

Madonna: Sometimes better. I've only *kissed* women, though. I've certainly had fantasies of [having sex with] women, but I'm not a lesbian.

❤

We saw his [Arnold Schwarzenegger's] beautiful new daughter up there at Camp David. I bent over to kiss her and she tried to bench-press me.

GEORGE BUSH

❤

I was on the front page of the *New York Times* kissing Jimmy Durante's nose.

PEGGY LEE

❤

Why is it that people are willing to go to a movie and watch someone get blown to bits for no reason and nobody wants to see two girls kissing or two men snuggling?

MADONNA

❤

I remember one time there was an article written about me, and I was kissing this woman and it said, "Cher Leaves Sonny for Another Woman." But, you know, what they neglected to say was that it was my sister in the picture.

CHER

I was afraid you might think you had to kiss me.

BARBARA BUSH, RUNNING PAST MISTLETOE IN THE WHITE HOUSE

I remember how people who smoke smelled when I kissed them. Like an old sewer.

CAROL CHANNING

The next night my life with Charlie [MacArthur] began. Everyone else had gone to bed and we were together on the outdoor swing. "You know, Helen, I want more than a stolen kiss," he said. "I want all of you." I would have done anything to keep him in my life. That was my blessed beautiful seduction, and to this day I thank God for it.

HELEN HAYES

You don't have to run from me. You can give me my hugs, my high fives, my kisses.

MAGIC JOHNSON

All my life I had wondered about my father. I had made him out to be a princely, gentle man, yet he never kissed me or showed any interest in me.

GERMAINE GREER

I don't think I could kiss a man who was a meat-eater.

LINDA McCARTNEY

I married the first boy I ever kissed.

BARBARA BUSH

He [Stallone's son Sage, age thirteen] wants to know how to soul kiss. I'm thinking about God, and he wants to know how to give a hickey.

SYLVESTER STALLONE

There was some actor that once said about me that kissing me was like kissing Hitler. Well, I think that's *his* problem. If I have to do intimate love scenes with somebody who really has these kinds of feelings toward me, then my fantasy can come into play. In other words, out with him, in with my fantasy. He was never there.

MARILYN MONROE

KISSING APHORISMS

*F*reud's great disciple Wilhelm Reich once said that in even the most outlandish statement there resides a grain of truth. Nowhere does this apply more forcefully than to the following aphorisms, pithy sayings that instruct or give insight into the intimate art of kissing. It might be worthwhile to meditate on one for a while and then, perhaps, put its precepts into practice . . .

Stealing a kiss may be petty larceny but sometimes it's also grand.

ANONYMOUS

Kissing a girl is like opening a jar of olives—hard to get the first one, but the rest come easy.

ANONYMOUS

A kiss of the mouth often touches not the heart.

H.G. BOHN (1796–1884), *HAND-BOOK OF PROVERBS*

Apple pie without the cheese is like a kiss without a squeeze.
NEIL SHAW, CANADIAN CHAIRMAN OF TATE & LYLE

Happiness is like a kiss—in order to get any good out of it you have to give it to somebody else.

ANONYMOUS

We are all mortal until the first kiss and the second glass of wine.
EDUARDO GALEANO, *THE BOOK OF EMBRACES*

Kissing a smoker is like licking an ashtray.
BUMPER STICKER

Kissing your hand may make you feel very very good but a diamond and safire bracelet lasts forever.
ANITA LOOS, *GENTLEMEN PREFER BLONDES* (1925).

People that bite the hand that feeds them usually kiss the boot that kicks them.
ERIC HOFFER (1902–1983), LONGSHOREMAN AND PHILOSOPHER

Like the girls you first kissed, the first cars you drive hold the sweetest memories.

AUTOWEEK

Stolen kisses are sweet.
OLD PROVERB

A legal kiss is never as good as a stolen one.
GUY DE MAUPASSANT (1850–1893), *A WIFE'S CONFESSION*

The sound of a kiss is not so loud as that of a cannon, but its echo lasts a great deal longer.
OLIVER WENDELL HOLMES, SR. (1809–1894), *THE PROFESSOR AT THE BREAKFAST-TABLE*

Kissing don't last: cookery do.
GEORGE MEREDITH (1828–1909), *THE ORDEAL OF RICHARD FEVEREL*

She that will kiss, they say, will do worse.
ROBERT DAVENPORT (1623–1639), *CITY NIGHT CAP*

Kisses are keys; wanton kisses are keys of sin.
NICHOLAS BRETON, *CROSSING OF PROVERBS* (1616)

Do not make me kiss, and you will not make me sin.
H. G. BOHN (1796–1884), *HAND-BOOK OF PROVERBS*

Some say kissing is a sin; but if it was not lawful, lawyers would not allow it; if it was not holy, ministers would not do it; if it was not modest, maidens would not take it; if it was not plenty, pure folk would not get it.

ROBERT BURNS (1756–1796)

♥

Alas! that women do not know
Kisses make men loath to go.

ANONYMOUS

♥

Many a miss would not be a missus
If liquor did not add a spark to her kisses.

E.L.C., *LISTEN* (*LIFE*, MARCH 1933)

♥

He is a fool that kisseth the maid when he may kiss the mistress.

JAMES HOWELL (1594?–1666), *PROVERBS*

♥

An intelligent girl is one who knows how to refuse a kiss without being deprived of it.

ANONYMOUS

♥

There is always one who kisses and one who only allows the kiss.

GEORGE BERNARD SHAW (1856–1950), *MAN AND SUPERMAN*

♥

Never a tear bedims the eye
That time and patience will not dry;
Never a lip is curved with pain
That can't be kissed into smiles again.

BRET HARTE (1836–1902), *THE LOST GALLEON*

❤

You can't kiss a girl unexpectedly—only sooner than she thought you would.

JACK SEAMAN

❤

Nobody wants to kiss when they are hungry.

DOROTHY DIX (1861–1951), AMERICAN JOURNALIST

❤

Everybody winds up kissing the wrong person goodnight.

ANDY WARHOL, *FROM A TO B & BACK AGAIN* (1975)

❤

A man may sometimes be forgiven the kiss to which he is not entitled, but never the kiss he has not the initiative to claim.

ARTHUR MORTIMER, *KISSES AND OTHER NONSENSE*

❤

SAD KISSES

Not all kissing is joyful. When a kiss stirs up sadness or happens in a sorrowful context it can be a bittersweet experience and can even cause pain. This chapter celebrates that melancholy aspect of kissing. And because parting is such sweet sorrow, we've included a subsection on goodbye kisses.

❤

Lips that taste of tears, they say
Are the best for kissing.
DOROTHY PARKER (1893—1967), *THRENODY*

❤

Though I know he loves me,
Tonight my heart is sad;
His kiss was not so wonderful
As all the dreams I had.
SARA TEASDALE (1884—1933), AMERICAN POET,
"THE KISS," *HELEN OF TROY*

❤

Dear as remember'd kisses after death,
And sweet as those by hopeless fancy feign'd
On lips that are for others.

TENNYSON (1809–1892), *THE PRINCESS*

Thus with a kiss I die.
SHAKESPEARE, *ROMEO AND JULIET* (ROMEO)

Alas! how easily things go wrong!
A sigh too much or a kiss too long,
And there follows a mist and a weeping rain,
And life is never the same again.

GEORGE MACDONALD (1824–1905), *PHANTASTES*

Here hung those lips that I have kissed.
SHAKESPEARE (HAMLET, AS HE REGARDS THE SKULL OF HIS FRIEND YORICK)

Blush, happy maiden, when you feel
The lips which press love's glowing seal;
But as the slow years darklier roll,
Grown wiser, the experienced soul
Will own as dearer far than they
The lips which kiss the tears away.

ELIZABETH AKERS ALLEN (1832–1911), *KISSES*

GOODBYE KISSES

One fond kiss before we part,
Drop a tear and bid adieu.
ROBERT DODSLEY (1703–1764), *THE PARTING KISS*

♥

One kiss more, and so farewell.
ANONYMOUS

♥

That farewell kiss which resembled greeting, that last glance of
love which becomes the sharpest pang of sorrow.
GEORGE ELIOT (1819–1880)

♥

HUMOROUS KISSES

When your kissing gets too serious—and, honestly, everyone suffers from this problem at times—it can cause your partner to lose interest. No one likes a stuffed shirt, especially in the bedroom. Luckily the solution to the problem is rather easy. If you find yourself boring someone with the same old kissing routine, try lightening the mood with a joke or some kissing humor. Most of the following quips, anecdotes, and stories will get a laugh out of your lover, after which you can rejoin the battle with uplifted mood, renewed gusto, and levity.

Any man who can drive safely while kissing a pretty girl is simply not giving the kiss the attention it deserves.

ANONYMOUS

I wasn't kissing her. I was whispering in her mouth.

CHICO MARX (REPLYING TO HIS WIFE,
WHO CAUGHT HIM KISSING A CHORUS GIRL)

He was kissing my feet and saying "Please, miss, don't give me a ticket, please." I said, "Get up. Are you trying to embarrass me? Well, it's working." I canceled his ticket.

NATALIE DANDURAND, PARKING CONTROL AGENT

Is kissing dirty? Only if you do it right.

WOODY ALLEN

Men seldom make passes
At girls who wear glasses.

DOROTHY PARKER (1893–1967), *NEWS ITEM*

Men who never make passes at women with glasses are asses.

LETTY COTTIN POGREBIN

Left-handers are better lovers than right-handers . . . I have heard this from many women who have been kissed from the right and from the left. Left-handers hold women as if they mean it.

ART BUCHWALD

I want to kiss you not because I find you beautiful, which I do; not because I admire what you've done or your intelligence, both of which I do; but because kissing you would be like kissing the American Stock Exchange, which I have always held in the highest esteem.

BROKER TO LAURA PEDERSEN, AUTHOR OF *PLAY MONEY: MY BRIEF BUT BRILLIANT CAREER ON WALL STREET*

Q: Does your wife mind kissing you with that beard?
A: Not at all. She's happy to go through a forest to get to a picnic.

ARCHIE MOORE, FORMER LIGHT-HEAVYWEIGHT CHAMP

Maybe we'll try a New Year's kiss, sort of coaxially.

JAY LENO (ON COHOSTING THE *TONIGHT* SHOW FROM THE WEST COAST WITH
JANE PAULEY IN THE EAST)

You kiss by the book.

SHAKESPEARE, *ROMEO AND JULIET* (JULIET)

B: Who was that guy I saw you kissing backstage?
A: Oh, I don't know.
B: You mean, you kiss a guy and you don't know who he is?
A: Well, I was standing in the wings, and he said, "How about
   you and me having a bite tonight?" And I said, "No, I'm busy
   tonight, but if you'd like I'll bite you now."

GEORGE BURNS AND GRACIE ALLEN

Lombardo started playing "Auld Lang Syne," and we stood in the
middle of the dance floor and kissed. She had to kiss me back;
we didn't have the kids so she had no one to call.

GEORGE BURNS (ON KISSING GRACIE ALLEN)

Says he, "I'd better call agin";
   Says she, "Think likely, mister!"
Thet last word pricked him like a pin,
   An' . . . Wal, he up an' kist her.

JAMES RUSSELL LOWELL (1819–1891, *THE COURTIN'*

The kiss originated when the first male reptile licked the first female reptile, implying in a subtle, complimentary way that she was as succulent as the small reptile he had for dinner the night before.

F. SCOTT FITZGERALD (1896–1940)

Formerly a kiss used to follow a nice evening, but nowadays a nice evening follows a kiss.

ANONYMOUS

It takes a lot of experience for a girl to kiss like a beginner.

ANONYMOUS

The doctor must have put [my pacemaker] in wrong. Every time my husband kisses me, the garage door goes up.

MINNIE PEARL

LITERARY KISSES

When they're not trying to be witty or ironically perverse, literary people often tend to delve more deeply than anyone else into the feelings that kisses arouse. Perhaps the best thing about most of the following quotes is that they'll give you ideas about the kinds of emotions you may experience while kissing.

♥

He knew that when he kissed this girl, his mind would never romp again like the mind of God . . . Then he kissed her. At his lips' touch she blossomed for him like a flower and the incarnation was complete.

F. SCOTT FITZGERALD, *THE GREAT GATSBY*

♥

She felt a little stir of something that came over her like a flush, a sort of inner buoyancy, and she lifted her face to kiss the warm blade of his cheekbone.

ANNE TYLER, *BREATHING LESSONS*

I wanted to kiss this woman so bad, I wondered how I would stay alive without it.

RICHARD COHEN, *SAY YOU WANT ME*

He put his mouth on my hot skin, drawing out the pain of the hangover. It felt as if his lips were sinking into my flesh, probing each cell for its wrongness and righting it. The medicine of the kiss healed me; then the kiss grew stronger, bringing me the exquisite sensual joy of the queen of the roses sucked by a bee.

MARGARET DIEHL, *MEN*

I grew up kissing books and bread . . . All this happened before I had ever kissed a girl. In fact . . . once I started kissing girls, my activities with regard to bread and books lost some of their special excitement.

SALMAN RUSHDIE, *IMAGINARY HOMELANDS*

She really wasn't any raving beauty, but she had a sulky look to her, and her lips stuck out in a way that made me want to mash them in for her.

JAMES M. CAIN, *THE POSTMAN ALWAYS RINGS TWICE*

None of the Victorian mothers—and most of the mothers were Victorian—had any idea how casually their daughters were accustomed to be kissed.

F. SCOTT FITZGERALD, *THIS SIDE OF PARADISE*

Lord, I wonder what fool it was that first invented kissing!

JONATHAN SWIFT (1667–1745)

Kissing is our greatest invention.

TOM ROBBINS, INTRODUCTION TO *A KISS IS JUST A KISS*

Come and kiss me, darling, before your body rots and worms pop in and out of your eye sockets.

NOEL COWARD, *PRIVATE LIVES*

I understand thy kisses, and thou mine.

SHAKESPEARE, *HENRY IV, PART I*

I never liked your manner toward me better than when you kissed me last.

SIR THOMAS MORE (IN A LETTER TO HIS DAUGHTER MARGARET ROPER ON THE EVE OF HIS EXECUTION)

He glared at her a moment through the dusk, and the next instant she felt his arms about her and his lips on her own lips. His kiss was like white lightning, a flash that spread, and spread again, and stayed.

HENRY JAMES, *THE PORTRAIT OF A LADY*

Being kissed . . . was something done to her, like the shampoos her mother used to give her at the kitchen sink.

JOHN UPDIKE

As he bent his head to come at her cheek she raised herself on tiptoe, and more by luck than good management touched his lips with her own. He jerked back as if he tasted the spider's poison, then he tipped his head forward before he could lose her, tried to say something against the sweet shut mouth, and in trying to answer she parted it. Her body seemed to lose all its bones, become fluid, a warm melting darkness . . .

COLLEEN McCULLOUGH, *THE THORN BIRDS*

I struggled to get away, and yet did it but faintly neither, and he held me fast, and still kissed me, till he was almost out of breath, and then, sitting down, says, "Dear Betty, I am in love with you."

DANIEL DEFOE (1660–1731), *MOLL FLANDERS*

Suddenly she lifted her mouth to be kissed. Her lips were taut and quivering and strenuous, his were soft, deep and delicate . . .

"Your mouth is so hard," he said, in faint reproach.

"And yours is so soft and nice," she said gladly.

"But why do you always grip your lips?" he asked, regretful.

"Never mind," she said swiftly. "It is my way."

RUPERT BIRKIN AND URSULA BRANGWEN IN D. H. LAWRENCE'S

WOMEN IN LOVE

I answer his fourth or fifth kiss. I begin to feel drunk . . . He teases me. He bites my ears and kisses me, and I like his fierceness. He throws me on the couch for a moment, but somehow I escape. I am aware of his desire. I like his mouth and the knowing force of his arms, but his desire frightens me, repulses me. I think it's because I don't love him.

ANAÏS NIN (1903–1977), *HENRY AND JUNE*

I dreamt my lady came and found me dead, . . .
And breathed such life with kisses in my lips,
That I revived, and was an emperor.

SHAKESPEARE, *ROMEO AND JULIET* (ROMEO)

I looked in her eyes and put my arm around her as I had before and kissed her. I kissed her hard and held her tight and tried to open her lips; they were closed tight . . . I held her close against me and could feel her heart beating and her lips opened and her head went back against my hand and then she was crying on my shoulder.

ERNEST HEMINGWAY, *A FAREWELL TO ARMS* (FREDERIC KISSES CATHERINE
AFTER SHE HAS SLAPPED HIM)

The lieutenant drew his wife close and kissed her vehemently. As their tongues explored each other's mouths, reaching out into the smooth, moist interior, they felt as if the still-unknown agonies of death had tempered their senses to the keenness of red-hot steel. The agonies they could not yet feel, the distant pains of death, had refined their awareness of pleasure.

YUKIO MISHIMA, *PATRIOTISM* (A STORY ABOUT A JAPANESE LIEUTENANT AND HIS
WIFE WHO COMMIT SUICIDE TOGETHER AT THE PEAK OF THEIR LIVES)

POETIC KISSES

A few of these poems are light and humorous, but most contain undercurrents of deep emotion. If you like to memorize quotes, the rhyme and meter will help you remember phrases that may come in handy when you break off from a kiss to whisper something sweet in your partner's ear. But if you haven't got time to learn any by heart, don't worry. After all, what could be more romantic than reading kissing poems to your lover?

She kissed his brow, his cheek, his chin,
And where she ends she doth anew begin.

SHAKESPEARE, *VENUS AND ADONIS*

Had she come all the way for this,
To part at last without a kiss?

WILLIAM MORRIS (1834–1896), *THE HAYSTACK IN THE FLOODS*

Kiss me, though you make me believe;
Kiss me, though I almost know
You are kissing to deceive.

ALICE CARY (1820–1871), AMERICAN POET, *MAKE BELIEVE*

Learn a little patience If you see Apocalypse or a flying saucer if you feel a little bliss give your wife a kiss you can't think straight it's never too late

ALLEN GINSBURG, *DO THE MEDITATION ROCK*

Give them thy fingers, me thy lips to kiss.

SHAKESPEARE, SONNET 128

Golden slumbers kiss your eyes,
Smiles awake you when you rise;
Sleep, pretty wantons, do not cry,
And I will sing a lullaby.

THOMAS DEKKER (1572?–1632), *THE PLEASANT COMEDY OF PATIENT GRISILL*

A kiss is but a kiss now! and no wave
Of a great flood that whirls me to the sea.

GEORGE MEREDITH (1829–1909), *MODERN LOVE*

Drink to me only with thine eyes,
And I will pledge with mine;
Or leave a kiss but in the cup,
And I'll not look for wine.

BEN JONSON (1573–1637), *TO CELIA*

Stolen sweets are always sweeter,
Stolen kisses much completer,
Stolen looks are nice in chapels,
Stolen, stolen, be your apples.

LEIGH HUNT (1784—1859), *SONG OF FAIRIES ROBBING AN ORCHARD*

Jenny kissed me when we met,
Jumping from the chair she sat in;
Time, you thief, who love to get
Sweets into your list, put that in.
Say I'm weary, say I'm sad,
Say that health and wealth have missed me;
Say I'm growing old, but add
Jenny kissed me.

LEIGH HUNT (1784—1859)

Like Dian's kiss, unasked, unsought,
Love gives itself, but is not bought.

LONGFELLOW (1807—1882), *ENDYMION*

I dare not ask a kiss;
I dare not beg a smile;
Lest having that, or this,
I might grow proud the while.

No, no, the utmost share
Of my desire, shall be
Only to kiss that air,
That lately kissed thee.

ROBERT HERRICK (1591—1674) *TO ELECTRA*

A man may drink and no be drunk;
 A man may fight and no be slain;
A man may kiss a bonnie lass,
 And aye be welcome back again.
ROBERT BURNS (1756–1796), *DUNCAN DAVISON*

The minister kiss'd the fiddler's wife,
 An' could na preach for thinkin' o't.
ROBERT BURNS (1756–1796), *MY LOVE SHE'S BUT A LASSIE YET*

He who binds to himself a joy
Does the winged life destroy
But he who kisses the joy as it flies
Lives in eternity's sun rise
WILLIAM BLAKE (1757–1827), ETERNITY

What of soul was left, I wonder, when the kissing had to stop?
ROBERT BROWNING (1812–1889), *TOCCATA OF GALUPPI'S*

And if he needs must kiss and tell,
I'll kick him headlong into hell.
NATHANIEL COTTON (1705–1788), *BURLESQUE UPON BURLESQUE*

Sweet Helen, make me immortal with a kiss!
Her lips suck forth my soul: see, where it flies!
CHRISTOPHER MARLOWE (1564–1593), *FAUSTUS*

Rose kissed me today,
　Will she kiss me tomorrow?
Let it be as it may,
Rose kissed me today.

AUSTIN DOBSON (1840–1921), *A KISS*

Whene'er I view those lips of thine,
　Their hue invites my fervent kiss;
Yet I forego that bliss divine,
　Alas, it were unhallow'd bliss!

BYRON (1788–1824), *TO M.S.G.* (M.S.G. WAS A MARRIED WOMAN.)

Gin a body meet a body
　Commin' through the rye,
Gin a body kiss a body,
　Need a body cry?

ROBERT BURNS (1756–1796), *BONNIE PEGGY ALISON*

Love in her sunny eyes does basking play;
Love walks the pleasant mazes of her hair;
Love does on both her lips for ever stray;
And sews and reaps a thousand kisses there.
In all her outward parts Love's always seen;
But, oh, he never went within.

ABRAHAM COWLEY (1618–1667), *THE CHANGE*

The kiss you take is better than you give;
Therefore no kiss.

SHAKESPEARE, *HENRY VIII*

I

I fear thy kisses, gentle maiden.
  Thou needest not fear mine;
My spirit is too deeply laden
  Ever to burthen thine.

II

I fear thy mien, thy tones, thy motion,
  Thou needest not fear mine;
Innocent is the heart's devotion
  With which I worship thine.

SHELLEY (1792–1822), TO ——

♥

It was thy kiss, Love, that made me immortal.

MARGARET WITTER FULLER (1810–1850), AMERICAN POET, *DRYAD SONG*

♥

What is love? 'tis not hereafter;
Present mirth hath present laughter;
What's to come is still unsure:
In delay there lies no plenty;
Then come kiss me, sweet and twenty,
Youth's a stuff will not endure.

SHAKESPEARE, *TWELFTH NIGHT*

♥

Oh! might I kiss those eyes of fire,
A million scarce would quench desire:
Still would I steep my lips in bliss,
And dwell an age on every kiss;
Nor then my soul should sated be,
Still would I kiss and cling to thee:
Nought should my kiss from thine dissever;
Still would we kiss, and kiss for ever,
E'en though the numbers did exceed
The yellow harvest's countless seed.
To part would be a vain endeavor:
Could I desist?—ah! never—never!

BYRON (1788–1824), *TO ELLEN*

"May I print a kiss on your lips?" I said,
    And she nodded her full permission;
So we went to press and I rather guess
    We printed a full edition.

JOSEPH LILIENTHAL, *A FULL EDITION*

SENSUAL KISSES

*Y*ou may think that the most arousing sexual acts occur after kissing. But for many people, kissing is the highest sensual pleasure. These quotes celebrate the passion and excitement of kissing and may inspire you to engage in some sensual kisses of your own.

♥

Often, very often, when her face was close to my lips, I felt the most ardent temptation to smother her with kisses . . . But I kept sufficient command over myself to avoid the slightest contact, for I was conscious that even one kiss would have been the spark which would have blown up all the edifice of my reserve. Every time she left me I remained astounded at my own victory, but, always eager to win fresh laurels, I longed for the following morning, panting for a renewal of this sweet yet very dangerous contest.

CASANOVA (1725-1798), *THE MEMOIRS OF JACQUES CASANOVA*, TRANSLATED BY ARTHUR MACHEN (1928) VOL. 1 (THIS EXCERPT DESCRIBES THE SIXTEEN-YEAR-OLD CASANOVA'S LOVE OF FOURTEEN-YEAR-OLD LUCIE DA PAESANO.)

♥

He was kissing her now and his mustache tickled her mouth, kissing her with slow, hot lips that were so leisurely as though he had the whole night before him. Charles had never kissed her like this. Never had the kisses of the Tarleton and Calvert boys made her go hot and cold and shaky like this. He bent her body backward and his lips traveled down her throat to where the cameo fastened her basque.

MARGARET MITCHELL, *GONE WITH THE WIND* (RHETT BUTLER KISSES SCARLETT

O'HARA BEFORE GOING OFF TO JOIN THE CONFEDERATE ARMY.)

His kisses were paralyzing her. She lay back, eyes closed and let him open her tight lace blouse, let him loosen the hooks of her skirt. Luxuriating in this helplessness, she let him rip away the chemise and the corset . . . Regal he seemed, his chest gleaming in the light.

ANN RICE, *THE MUMMY*

[He] would . . . kiss me hard,
As if he plucked up kisses by the roots
That grew upon my lips.
SHAKESPEARE, *OTHELLO*

♥

Graze on my lips, and when those mounts are dry,
Stray lower, where the pleasant fountains lie.
GERVASE MARKHAM AND LEWIS MACHIN, *THE DUMB KNIGHT* (1608)

♥

I was making love to a man, a man I hardly even know. He was kissing the face off me and I was kissing the face off him. And I found it highly satisfactory.

ANITA LOOS (1888–1981), AMERICAN PLAYWRIGHT AND SCREENWRITER,
HAPPY BIRTHDAY

I clasp thy waist; I feel thy bosom's beat.
O, kiss me into faintness, sweet and dim.

ALEXANDER SMITH (1830–1867), SCOTTISH POET

I want to kiss your lips, first gently, hardly touching, then with the flame of passion.

INCURABLE ROMANTIX OF NEW YORK, A COMPANY THAT GHOST-WRITES LOVE
LETTERS

Listen here, Babycakes, I love everything about you. I'd love to kiss your lips, chest, stomach . . . I have juices so hot I can barely breathe.

FAN LETTER TO RICHARD GRIECO, STAR OF FOX'S *21 JUMP STREET*

Rearing up with a swift, silent movement, she pounced on me, mastering me with a fantastically soft mouth and an arm around my neck. Above my own, her wide-open eyes listened to the retreating footsteps and her free hand, held high, marked the rhythm of her husband's walk and of the quivering of her own lips that seemed to be counting my heart-beats: one, two, three, four, five.

COLETTE (1873–1954), *CLAUDINE MARRIED*, TRANSLATED BY ANTONIA WHITE

But his mouth was already slanting across hers, and he'd already ensured there'd be no escape from it. Leisurely, with infinite care, he bestowed on her the finesse of a lifetime, kisses meant to entice, to mesmerize, to tap every sensual impulse she possessed. Her arms were already encircling his neck when his tongue seduced her lips to part, entered, and took her swiftly to that realm of not-caring-what-he-did.

JOHANNA LINDSEY, *GENTLE ROGUE* (1990)

He could not have known that I had not kissed a man before. Everything I did, every motion of my body as I arched it up against his, came from something, some primitive instinct beyond myself. That afternoon I was no sixteen-year-old girl; I was a woman—*female*—exulting in the feeling of power I had suddenly discovered I could wield.

ROSEMARY ROGERS, *THE WANTON* (1985)

He moved closer and in a rapid movement slipped his arm about her narrow waist, nearly lifting her from the floor, and then covered her mouth with his . . . She was too surprised to resist and hung limp in his embrace . . . She was left breathless each time his mouth took hers and passionate kisses seemed to cover her face and bosom.

KATHLEEN E. WOODIWISS, *THE FLAME AND THE FLOWER* (1972)

His mouth came down over hers in a hard, angry kiss that took her breath away. There was no gentleness in him, no tenderness. His arms held her pinned against the length of his body, and he kissed her savagely and thoroughly, his tongue raping her mouth until she felt she would swoon, felt her legs become weak, felt a strange, feverish pounding in her temples that seemed to spread through her whole body and engulf her.

ROSEMARY ROGERS, *SWEET SAVAGE LOVE* (1975)

Then she threw her head and bosom back, and melting, as it were, in one great bodily caress, she rubbed her cheeks coaxingly first against one shoulder then against the other. Her lustful mouth breathed desire over her limbs. She put out her lips, kissed herself long and long in the neighborhood of her armpit, and laughed at the other Nana who, also, was kissing herself in the mirror.

EMILE ZOLA (1840–1902), *NANA*

The first kiss I gave them was prompted by entirely harmless motives . . . but those innocent kisses, as we repeated them, very soon became ardent ones, and kindled a flame which certainly took us by surprise, for we stopped, as by common consent, after a short time, looking at each other very much astonished and rather serious . . . It was natural that the burning kisses I had given and received should have sent through me the fire of passion, and that I should suddenly have fallen madly in love with the two charming sisters.

CASANOVA (1725–1798), *THE MEMOIRS OF JACQUES CASANOVA*, TRANSLATED BY ARTHUR MACHEN (1928) VOL. 1 (THIS EXCERPT DESCRIBES THE BEGINNING OF HIS SEDUCTION OF THE ORPHANED SISTERS NANETTE AND MARTON.)

KISSES FROM
AROUND THE WORLD

*C*ount your blessings if you live in a country where public kissing is allowed. In Malaysia you could be fined seventy-five dollars for a public kiss. In 1990, 764 couples were fined by Kuala Lumpur's City Municipal Council for kissing, embracing, and other "indecent behavior" in public parks.

Recently in Cairo, Egypt, a plumber and his fiancée were jailed for twenty-four hours in separate jails for kissing in open court. Nearly ninty percent of the Bangladeshi population are followers of Islam, which among other things forbids drinking or kissing in public. And kissing is rarely allowed in films made in India.

You may want to keep these facts in mind when planning a romantic getaway, say a honeymoon, abroad . . .

AFGHANISTAN

We have a saying in Afghanistan that you can't send a kiss through a messenger.

FAREED MAZDAK, WATAN (HOMELAND) PARTY'S DEPUTY CHAIRMAN AND THIRD MOST POWERFUL OFFICIAL

AUSTRIA

I kiss your hand, gracious lady.
(*Küss die Hand, gnädige Frau.*)
AUSTRIAN GREETING

CHINA

Husbands only think of themselves, and so there's no kissing or hugging.

LIU DALIN, PRESIDENT OF THE SHANGHAI SEX EDUCATION RESEARCH SOCIETY

China has no legal definition of pornography, and anything showing a naked body or even kissing can be considered obscene.

LOS ANGELES TIMES

DENMARK

Kisses are the messengers of love.
DANISH PROVERB

Many kiss the babe for the nurse's sake.
DANISH PROVERB

Who takes the child by the hand takes the mother by the heart.
(*Hvo der tager Barnet ved Haanden tager Moderen ved Hjertet.*)

DANISH PROVERB

ENGLAND

They kiss you when you arrive, they kiss you when you go away, and they kiss you when you return. Go where you will, it is all kissing.

ERASMUS (1466?–1536), DESCRIBING HIS EXPERIENCES WITH ENGLISHWOMEN

If we want to hug or kiss, we always do that in private. Other people have other things, but this is just a fact of life for us.

DUCHESS OF YORK, ON KISSING THE DUKE OF YORK

Wishing myself (specially an evening) in my sweetheart's arms, whose pretty dukkys [breasts] I trust shortly to kiss. Written with the hand of him that was, is and shall be yours by his will. H.R.

KING HENRY VIII TO HIS THEN-MISTRESS ANNE BOLEYN IN 1528

You have to kiss a lot of frogs to find a prince.

PHRASE EMBROIDERED ON A SILK CUSHION ON PRINCESS DIANA'S BED

Your old granny and subject must be the first to kiss your hand.

QUEEN MARY TO PRINCESS ELIZABETH, FEBRUARY 1952, JUST BEFORE SHE
BECAME QUEEN ELIZABETH II

A many kisses he did give:
And I returned the same
Which made me willing to receive
That which I dare not name.

APHRA BEHN (1640—1689), ENGLISH POET AND NOVELIST, *THE DUTCH LOVER*,
"THE WILLING MISTRESS"

ESKIMO KISSES

Two [Eskimo travelers] would greet each other in the traditional manner by rubbing noses together.

ASEN BALIKCI, *THE NETSILIK ESKIMO* (1970)

FRANCE

What I like about France is the kissing—one of civilization's finest achievements.

ISABEL HUGGAN

Only you can restore me to happiness. Tell me that you love me, that you love me alone! That will make me the happiest of women . . . Adieu, I send you a thousand tender kisses—and I am yours, all yours.

JOSEPHINE DE BEAUHARNAIS, WIFE OF NAPOLEON BONAPARTE (IN A LETTER TO HER TWENTY-FOUR-YEAR-OLD LOVER, LIEUTENANT HIPPOLYTE CHARLES)

Some fine night the doors will open, and there I'll be . . . I hope before long to crush you with a million kisses burning as though beneath the equator.

NAPOLEON BONAPARTE (IN A LETTER TO HIS WIFE JOSEPHINE)

A kiss on the heart, another a little lower, another lower still, far lower.

NAPOLEON (IN A LETTER TO JOSEPHINE)

In France, as I learned only last week, the choice as to whether to give two or three kisses on the cheek was originally an indicator of a Catholic or Protestant upbringing.

ELEANOR IRONSIDE

In every love affair, there is one who kisses, and one who turns the cheek.

OLD FRENCH PROVERB

I have a right to kiss on two cheeks because I speak French. But I only kiss on one cheek because we live in America.

CHRISTY FERER, FASHION EDITOR OF WNBC-TV

You will notice how sweetly the young [in France] greet one another, with little pecking kisses planted on both cheeks.

ANGELA LAMBERT

Lovers can live on kisses and cool water.

OLD FRENCH SAYING

I was besieged everywhere I went. Even in the toilet I had to sign autographs. Men were kissing me on the cheeks on the streets of Paris.

WILLIAM CONRAD

♥

And in that first flame
Is all the nectar of the kiss.
(*Et c'est dans la première flamme*
Qu'est tout le nectar du baiser.)

PONCE-DENIS ÉCOUCHARD LEBRUN (1729–1807), *MES SOUVENIRS*

♥

It is not a fashion for the maids in France to kiss before they are married.

SHAKESPEARE, *HENRY V*

♥

Kiss of a sweetheart.
(Baiser de l'amourette.)

FRENCH PHRASE

♥

Kiss me again, rekiss me and kiss me;
Give me your raciest one;
Give me your most amorous one,
I'll give you back four hotter than fire.
(*Baise m'encor, rebaise-moi et baise;*
Donne-m'en un de tes plus savoureux;
Donne-m'en un de tes plus amoureux,
Je t'en rendrai quatre plus chauds que braise.)

LOUISE LABÉ (1524–1566), FRENCH POET, SONNET XVIII

A kiss that doesn't spring from love
Will never excite the mouth.
(*Baiser qui au coeur ne touche*
Ne fait rien qu'affadir la bouche.)

ADRIEN DE MONTLUC (1558-1646), *LA COMÉDIE DES PROVERBES*

GERMANY

He's [my boyfriend] promised me a kiss on the other side of the [Berlin] wall.

BRITTA KIEHEN, AGE NINETEEN

To help you get the best out of the Germans, here is a guide on how to deal with them. Do remember to shake hands. This especially applies at parties and receptions when you may say hello to hundreds of clenched fingers at once. Do not kiss hands unless you are at least two of the following: a) very confident; b) completely sober; c) a count.

DAVID MARSH, *FINANCIAL TIMES*

Tell me who first did kisses suggest?
It was a mouth all glowing and blest;
It kissed and it thought of nothing beside.

HEINRICH HEINE (1797–1856), *NEW SPRING: LYRICS*

One kiss from rosy lips and I fear neither storm nor rock!
(*Einer Kuss von rosiger Lippe,*
Und ich fürchte nicht Sturm nicht Klippe!)

GERMAN FOLK SONG

No one can forbid an honorable kiss.
(*Einer Kuss in Ehren kann niemand verwehren.*)
GERMAN PROVERB

❤

Oh they loved dearly; their souls kissed, they kissed with their eyes, they were both but one single kiss!
HEINE (1797—1856), *IDEAS*

❤

O what falsehood lies in kisses!
HEINE (1797—1856), *RETURN HOME*

❤

Short their words and long their kisses,
And their hearts are overflowing.
HEINE (1797—1856), *LYRICAL INTERLUDE: DONNA CLARA*

❤

Giving kisses, stealing kisses,
Is the world's chief occupation.
(*Küsse geben, Küsse rauben
Ist der Welt Beschäftigung.*)
LUDWIG CHRISTOPH HEINRICH HÖLTY (1748-1776), *MAILIED*

❤

What now avails my joy to me?
Like dreams the warmest kisses flee,
Like kisses, soon all joys are gone.
(Was hilft es mir, dass ich geniesse?
Wie Träume fliehn die wärmsten Küsse,
Und alle Freude wie ein Kuss.)

JOHANN WOLFGANG VON GOETHE (1749–1832), *LIEDER, GLÜCK UND TRAUM*

(TRANSLATED BY E. A. BOWRING)

GREECE

A kiss must last long to be enjoyed.

GREEK PROVERB

If you kiss me you hate me, and if you hate me you kiss me. But if you don't hate me, dear friend, don't kiss me!

NICARCHUS, GREEK EPIGRAMMATIC POET

HEBREW

The kisses of an enemy are deceitful.

BIBLE, PROVERBS 27:6

When a knave kisses you, count your teeth.

HEBREW PROVERB

HUNGARY

I kiss your hand.
(Kezet csokolom.)

HUNGARIAN GREETING

Good coffee should be black like the devil, hot like hell, and sweet like a kiss.

HUNGARIAN PROVERB

Frequent kisses end in a baby.

HUNGARIAN PROVERB

ICELAND

From a ship expect speed, from a shield cover,
Keenness from a sword, but a kiss from a girl.

THE WORDS OF THE HIGH ONE, A NINTH-CENTURY POEM OF MAXIMS
ATTRIBUTED TO THE GOD ODIN

INDIA

The following are the places for kissing: the forehead, the eyes, the cheeks, the throat, the bosom, the breast, the lips, and the interior of the mouth. Moreover, the people of the Lat country kiss also on the following places: the joints of the thighs, the arms, and the navel. But Vatsyayana thinks that though kissing is practiced by these people in the above places on account of the intensity of their love, and the customs of their country, it is not fit to be practiced by all.

THE KAMA SUTRA OF VATSYAYANA (TRANSLATED BY SIR RICHARD BURTON AND
F. F. ARBUTHNOT)

In India, couples who get carried away in public may find themselves in prison. Kissing in public is an offense and only recently have the nearly eight hundred Indian films made each year begun to show flashes of kissing.

GARGI PARSAI, *SEATTLE TIMES*

People from countries such as India and Pakistan, where even a kiss is not allowed in the cinema, find it hard to bring up their children in homes where television often shows the sexual act.

RICHARD WEST, *THE TIMES* (LONDON)

In India kissing is just not done.

MIRA NAIR, INDIAN DIRECTOR OF *SALAAM BOMBAY!*

He set my heart floating on the honey stream of his words,
With his amorous kiss he burnt my lips,
And left me utterly alone, and unfulfilled.

KSHETRAYYA, SEVENTEENTH-CENTURY INDIAN POET, "DANCING GIRL'S SONG,"
INDIAN LOVE POEMS (TRANSLATED BY TAMBIMUTTU AND R. APPALASWAMY)

IRELAND

Kiss me, I'm Irish!

IRISH SAYING

Though I am old with wandering
Through hollow lands and hilly lands,
I will find out where she has gone,
And kiss her lips and take her hands;
And walk among long dappled grass,
And pluck till time and times are done
The silver apples of the moon,
The golden apples of the sun.

WILLIAM BUTLER YEATS (1865–1939), *THE SONG OF WANDERING AENGUS*

Lyin' for a whole night stretched out on the side of a lonely counthry lane, with his head, his darlin' head, that I often kissed an' fondled, half hidden in the wather of a runnin' brook.

SEAN O'CASEY, *JUNO AND THE PAYCOCK* (1924)

Kiss the cook. She is Irish.

MAGNET ON STOVE

ITALY

This kiss, unbelievable. To me, it is one of my favorite scenes because it goes on so long that it will for sure get a reaction out of the public . . . I've done eleven films and he's [Pee-Wee Herman] the best I've kissed.

VALERIA GOLINO, ITALIAN ACTOR WHO STARRED IN *RAIN MAN* WITH DUSTIN
HOFFMAN AND TOM CRUISE, DISCUSSING HER THREE-MINUTE SIXTEEN-SECOND
KISSING SCENE IN *BIG TOP PEE-WEE*, WHICH TOOK SEVEN HOURS TO FILM

Unlike the United States, men do not stand when a women enters or leaves a room, and they do not kiss a women's hand. The latter is reserved for royalty.

KATHERINE M. GLOVER, *BUSINESS AMERICA*

Sweetest the kiss that's stolen from weeping maid.
(*Primus titubans audacia furtis.*)

CLAUDIAN (FLOURISHED 365–408), LATIN POET, *DE NUPTIS HONORII AUGUSTI*

I do not care for kisses unless I have snatched them in spite of resistance.
(*Basia dum nolo, nisi quae luctantia carpsi.*)

MARTIAL, *EPIGRAMS*

Give me another naughty naughty kiss before we part.
(*Da savium etiam prius quam abis.*)

PLAUTUS, *ASINARIA*

Take me by the earlaps and match my little lips to your little lips.
(*Prehende auriculis, compara labella cum labella.*)

PLAUTUS, *ASINARIA*

He who has taken kisses, if he take not the rest beside, will deserve to lose even what was granted.
(*Oscula qui sumpsit, si non et cetera sumet,/Haec quoque, quae data sunt, perdere dignus erit.*)

OVID, *THE ART OF LOVE*

He who shall never be separated from me kissed my mouth all trembling.
(*Questi, che mai da me non fia diviso,*
La bocca mi baciò tutto tremante.)

DANTE, *INFERNO*

The kiss of peace
(*Osculum pacis*)
(AT ONE TIME PART OF THE CELEBRATION OF MASS)

JAPAN

Battlefront brothels run by the Imperial Japanese Army in occupied Asian territories were operated under strict Army rules . . . The Army regulation stipulates that the hostesses (prostitutes) will not be kissed.

KYODO NEWS SERVICE

When I met people here [in the United States] it was kissing and hugging. In Japan, you just bow.

SEIKO, AGE TWENTY-EIGHT, JAPANESE SUPERSTAR SINGER

The Japanese never know when they are friendly enough to kiss.

JOSEPH P. BRUNETTO, PRESIDENT OF THE JAPAN-AMERICA SOCIETY OF
WESTCHESTER (ON JAPANESE GREETING CUSTOMS)

Kisses and embraces are unknown in Japan as tokens of affection except between mothers and little children. After babyhood, kissing is held to be highly immodest. Parents and children do not kiss; husbands and wives may meet after years of absence, yet they will only kneel down and salute each other, smile, and perhaps cry a little for joy. They never rush into each other's arms or utter phrases of affection, but show their love through acts of exquisite courtesy and kindness.

LAFCADIO HEARN, *OUT OF THE EAST*

JEWISH

Kissing is not customary among Jews. How does one, out of a clear sky, kiss, especially a child his father?

MENDELÉ (1837–1917), YIDDISH SATIRIST, *DOS VINTSHFINGERL*

Rather an honest slap than a false kiss.

YIDDISH PROVERB

Better a slap from the wise than a kiss from a fool.

YIDDISH PROVERB

The universe hangs on a kiss, exists in the hold of a kiss.

ZALMAN SHNEOR, HEBREW POET, *THE KISS* (1906)

Give your ear to all, your hand to a friend, but your mouth only to your wife.

YIDDISH PROVERB

KOREA

Fifteen years ago, there was not even kissing in Korean films. But now . . . Whoa!

SANG KU JOO, FORMER KOREAN SOLDIER

In an unprecedented move, North Korean Premier Yon Hung Muk was greeted with garlands of flowers and a kiss from a South Korean schoolgirl as he became the highest-ranking North Korean official to step across the heavily guarded Military Demarcation Line that separates North from South Korea.

TORONTO STAR

MALAYSIA

Rules against kissing exist because Malaysians are a prudish lot.

MAT SAAT ZAKI, PSYCHOLOGIST, NATIONAL UNIVERSITY OF MALAYSIA

Yes . . . Well . . . maybe it's embarrassing to other people. Maybe courting couples should be a bit more discreet . . . I don't know. But sometimes people just get carried away, you know.

RAZALI RAHMAN, AGE TWENTY-TWO, MALAYSIAN FACTORY TECHNICIAN (ON PUBLIC KISSING)

MALTA

Kisses are like almonds.

MALTESE PROVERB

MEXICO

Kisses are first, and cusses come later.
MEXICAN PROVERB

THE NETHERLANDS

Two kisses, one on each cheek, is a spreading European greeting between men and women . . . A third kiss for good measure is common in Belgium and in Holland's Catholic south (in the mainly Protestant north the Dutch make do with two).
THE ECONOMIST

My name is Popie Jopie
I happily travel round
And always when I arrive
I spontaneously kiss the ground.
DUTCH SMASH HIT RECORDING TAUNTING POPE JOHN PAUL II WHEN HE VISITED
THE NETHERLANDS IN 1985

PAKISTAN

Some Pakistanis are concerned that CNN broadcasts do not meet "Islamic decency standards" . . . A Pakistani censor scrambles and blacks out obvious problem material, such as kissing couples and scantily clad women.
HASAN M. JAFRI

PARAGUAY

Paraguayans kiss each other on the cheek just to say hello.
CARLOS GWYNN, OLYMPIC TENNIS COACH

PHILIPPINES

It is natural for a girl if she knows you even slightly to greet you with a kiss. In the Philippines, nobody would ever do that unless it was your wife. Here [in the U.S.A.] the girls give away a lot of free kisses.

ROBERT ESPANOL, PHILIPPINE IMMIGRANT

POLAND

It was once the custom of the Polish aristocracy—from which I am in part descended—to kiss a woman's knee as a sign of great respect . . . I just this week was informed, the knee kiss is supposed to be a friendly gesture reserved for little girls under the age of five.

MICHAEL KILIAN

I kiss your hands. I fall at your feet.

POLISH GREETING.

I have no regrets about my wife's absence, since I've got so many kisses over here that I have no space left on my cheeks.

LECH WALESA

ROMANIA

We kissed one another on the streets.

REZVAN MITROI, JOURNALIST (ON THE EUPHORIA IN ROMANIA AFTER DICTATOR NICOLAE CEAUSESCU WAS OVERTHROWN IN 1989)

♥

A cunning person's kiss is like that of a mosquito.
ROMANIAN PROVERB

RUSSIA

Kiss me, Comrade!
CAPTION ON SMUTTY POSTCARDS

My elbow is close, but I cannot kiss it.
RUSSIAN PROVERB

My physical memory was that she [my mother] was beautiful and perfumed. She used to stop in the evenings in my bedroom and would probably kiss me and touch me with her hands and then leave. Her fragrance would stay behind.
SVETLANA STALIN, STALIN'S DAUGHTER

What surprised me most is that it is so hard to tell the [U.S.A. and Soviet] kids apart. They all talk about music, divorce, school, dating, kissing.
MARLO THOMAS

SAUDI ARABIA

No kissing, please.
SAUDI CROWN PRINCE ABDULLAH TO PLO CHIEF YASSER ARAFAT

You cannot change relations . . . simply by kissing cheeks.
SAUDI POLITICAL ANALYST

A sponge to wipe out the past; a rose to make the present sweet;
and a kiss to salute the future.

ARABIC PROVERB

SOUTH AFRICA

I just had a wonderful call from Bishop Tutu. He said, "Nadine,
Mmm, mmm, mmm" (kissing over the phone). It was typically
Tutu.

NADINE GORDIMER

SPAIN

He that wipes the child's nose kisseth the mother's cheek.

SPANISH PROVERB

Many kiss the hand they wish cut off.

SPANISH PROVERB

A kiss without a mustache is like an egg without salt.

SPANISH PROVERB

One maxim keep in sight,
Ye courtiers, it is this:
That no one comes to kiss
Unless he means to bite.
([*Que*] *en la corte es menester*
Con este cuidado andar,
Que nadie llega á besar
Sin intento de morder.)

RUIZ DE ALARCON (1833–1891), MEXICAN-BORN SPANISH DRAMATIST, *LOS FAVORES DEL MUNDO*

SWEDEN

It was not to mama he wrote, it was to his former fiancée, his sweetheart . . . At the bottom of the page he put a star, as lovers do, and wrote beside it—just as of old—"Kiss here!" When he had finished and read through his letter, he felt a glow on his cheeks, and was somewhat embarrassed. Why, he could not exactly say. It was like giving out his innermost thoughts to some one who might perhaps not understand them.

Still, he sent the letter.

AUGUST STRINDBERG, *AUTUMN*

TURKEY

The state telephone company has banned all romantic words from pocket-pager subscribers. Words such as "love" and "kiss" are prohibited.

REUTERS

❤

When we were visiting one village, an elderly man came up to me and wanted to kiss my hand. I got a bit angry, and said, "You are older than I am. I should kiss your hand." But he replied, "I am not kissing your hand. I am kissing the hand of our struggle."

LEYLA ZANA, TURKISH POLITICIAN

VIETNAM

Even in love stories, they get some communism in there. Over there, they cannot even kiss. They just hold hands in front of a billboard of some leader.

PHAM, OWNER OF XUAN THU PRESS, A VIETNAMESE PRESS IN CALIFORNIA

♥

MISCELLANEOUS KISSES

*T*his chapter contains a little bit of everything, including quotations on animal kisses, philosophical kisses, advertising kisses, kissing diseases, and more.

THE BENEFITS OF KISSING

Everyone wants a hug and a kiss. It translates into every language and religion and is absolutely recession-proof.

> GEORGETTE MOSBACHER, CEO, LA PRAIRIE

A baby needs hugs, kisses, cuddling, and most of all love.

> SIGN POSTED IN A VIRGINIA PLAYGROUND

QUICK KISSING QUOTES

I feel great. I kiss pretty good too.

> T-SHIRT

Hugs and kisses . . . FREE
ENTRY ON CAFETERIA PRICE LIST

New Year's Resolution: "Get really kissed."
CLAUDIO PRESTO, GANNETT NEWS SERVICE

How Kissing Fits Into The Big Picture

Unless the game has changed since I was a girl, first base was
kissing; second base, petting above the waist; third base, petting
below the waist; and a home run meant going all the way.
DEAR ABBY

In sixth grade, first base is holding hands and second base is
kissing on the mouth.

ERICA BUEHRENS, AGE FOURTEEN, STUDENT AT HUNTER HIGH SCHOOL

Kids On Kissing

I'm not doing any kissing, and I'm not getting married, either. I
don't like it at all. If you start kissing, you'll end up doing a lot
of cleaning . . . The men go out and do anything they feel like and
leave us stuck in the house.
LORI, AGE EIGHT, *GROWING UP ISN'T HARD TO DO IF YOU START OUT AS A KID:*
CHILDREN'S CANDID VIEWS OF EVERYDAY LIFE, BY DAIVD HELLER

Kissing is not high on our class discussion list. When you mention
the word "kiss" the class goes hysterical and the teachers can't
control them.

DANNY GOLDSMITH, AGE NINE

My grandmother is very nice but she gives really big kisses that never end.

SARAH RYAN, SIXTH GRADER

KISSING WISHES

I wish I were small and cuddly, wore ruffles, and got kissed at parties.

ERMA J. FISK, AGE EIGHTY

May his soul be in heaven—he deserves it I'm sure—
Who was first the inventor of kissing.

ANONYMOUS

ANIMAL KISSES

A cat-kiss: A long, slow blink with your gaze and attention fixed on the cat's eyes, before, during and after the blink.

ANITA FRAZIER, *THE NATURAL CAT, A HOLISTIC GUIDE FOR FINICKY OWNERS*

Most of them [teddy bears] are cuddled or kissed on the nose so much that the nose gets dented in.

BUNNY CAMPIONE, APPRAISER FOR SOTHEBY'S

Who would refuse to kiss a lapdog, if it were preliminary to the lips of his lady?

WILLIAM CONGREVE (1670–1729), *THE OLD BACHELOR*

PHILOSOPHICAL KISSES

A kiss may not be the truth, but it is what we wish were true.

STEVE MARTIN, *L.A. STORY* (CAROLCO/INDIEPROD/LA FILMS, 1991)

It's taken me a lifetime to realize that people don't usually stay with those they kiss, caress, and fall in love with.

MARY MEYER, FOUNDER OF THE NATIONAL CHASTITY ASSOCIATION

Yet they that know all things but know
That all this life can give us is
A child's laughter, a woman's kiss.

YEATS (1865–1939), *BAILE AND AILLINN*

ADVERTISING KISSES

Nothing makes your heart beat faster than kissing a married man. A husband makes a better lover.

BMP DDB NEEDHAM, QUOTED IN *THE TIMES* (LONDON)

If he kisses you once, will he kiss you again?

CERTS COMMERCIAL

Without Chap Stick, going out in the sun is like kissing a light bulb.

CHAP STICK ADVERTISING SLOGAN

Clorets was created to do one thing, one thing only . . . make your breath "Kissing Sweet" . . . all you need do is chew Clorets and in seconds your breath becomes "Kissing Sweet," even after smoking, drinking, or eating onions . . . *Make this breath test.* Eat onions. Chew Clorets. Hear your best friend say, "Your breath is " 'Kissing Sweet.' "

ADVERTISEMENT IN *LIFE*, MAY 12, 1952

KISSING DISEASES

Kissing is a very inefficient way of transmitting a cold.

BRUCE FARBER, INFECTIOUS DISEASE SPECIALIST

From two to 250 germ colonies may switch sides during a kiss, but 95 percent are harmless . . . Women's lipsticks (and men's Chap Sticks) cut down the germ count, because most are made with a mild antiseptic, and the heavy base tends to suffocate the colonies.

TIME

Since man is a social creature, he must expect risks in social contact, even in petting parties. The only alternative is to become a hermit or a bore. Kissing can be not only a pleasant but a harmless pastime if ordinary lip and mouth hygiene is practiced.

DR. ARTHUR H. BRYAN, BACTERIOLOGIST

Kisses may not spread germs, but they certainly lower resistance.

LOUISE ERICKSON

MUSICAL KISSES

Musicians usually sing about kisses, but in these quotes they talk about them. And what they say should be music to every lover's ears.

It was an absolute mistake doing that scene. I was pressured into it, and won't do it again. I didn't touch her, I didn't kiss her, but I was in bed with her and that's not proper to me . . . They all have that stuff in it—bad language, sexual scenes, and nudity. It's got no class. I don't like kissing people I don't know. If they do that, they'll have to get a body double.

HARRY CONNICK, JR., NEW ORLEANS–BORN PIANIST/SINGER/COMPOSER
COMPLAINING ABOUT HIS SEX SCENE IN THE FILM *LITTLE MAN TATE*

Yeah, I know all my songs are about love and about hugging and kissing and squeezing and teasing. But when I'm on stage singing a song like "You're My Lady," sometimes I'll see a guy in the audience embracing his lady. And that really makes me feel good.

FREDDIE JACKSON

I used to bring like ten girls on stage and kiss 'em all. It wasn't a part of the show—one night I just did it. As to how serious the kisses were, I try to be fair but sometimes the fans get a little too generous with their kisses.

DONNIE WAHLBERG OF NEW KIDS ON THE BLOCK

♥

If I could get just one kiss from Joe, or Jordan, or any of them, I'd be willing to be single for the rest of my life. Really.

FAN OF NEW KIDS ON THE BLOCK

♥

I get touched and kissed and hugged by strangers a lot. It's a big burden sometimes. You feel like you don't want to let them down, but if you give them too much, you don't have anything left inside you.

KATHY MATTEA, COUNTRY VOCALIST

♥

Close the door when you get home from work, and hug and kiss with someone special for at least fifteen minutes—longer is better.

ANITA BAKER

♥

All the girls ran up and gave me a kiss and I thought, "Oh, wow. Is this all I have to do? This is wonderful." So I became a guitar player.

STEPHEN J. NICHOLAS OF NUAGE RECORDS

♥

I feel so good that I'm going to kiss myself.

JAMES BROWN

PROHIBITED KISSES

Nietzsche said that one way to discover the truth is to listen to liars and then believe the opposite of what they say. By the same reasoning, one way to discover exciting kissing practices and techniques is to listen to those who would prohibit kissing, and then . . . do just the opposite of what they suggest! In that spirit we offer the following regulations, prohibitions, and laws against kissing. Have fun breaking the rules!

There's a strict code of behavior students must follow on campus: No dancing. No kissing. No holding hands. And no "excessive familiarity"—cuddling or leaning on boyfriends or girlfriends.

    JAMES RAINEY (WRITING ABOUT PACIFIC COAST BAPTIST BIBLE COLLEGE)

Adultery or illicit sex must not be explicitly treated or justified or presented attractively. Excessive and lustful kissing, lustful embraces, suggestive postures and gestures are not to be shown.

    PROPOSED NEW MORAL CODE FOR MOVIES, ADVOCATED BY THE ATLANTA-
    BASED CHRISTIAN FILM AND TELEVISON COMMISSION

Those kissing while playing in a band are required to pause for breath between each kiss.

ATLANTA, GEORGIA, LAW

No couple, whether married or unmarried, may kiss during a concert or while a band is playing for longer than three minutes.

SIOUX FALLS, SOUTH DAKOTA, LAW

No one may kiss a woman while attending a concert, unless she's "properly chaperoned."

MADISON, WISCONSIN, LAW

It's recommended that there not be lot of kissing because that might lead to something else.

SCOTT BOYENGER, AGE NINETEEN, A MORMON

The kisses between a husband and a wife are hardly ever a mortal sin and most often not even a venial sin.

PALESTRA DEL CLERO (FORUM OF THE CLERGY), A ROMAN CATHOLIC

THEOLOGICAL PUBLICATION (1956)

If you walk down the street and see a man and woman kissing in a car, turn away, that's evil.

SISTER BEATRICE, *WASHINGTON POST*

KISSING TECHNIQUE

adonna brushed her teeth a few times before the cameras rolled for her *Saturday Night Live* kiss with comedian Mike Meyers—a sure sign of a good kisser, one who understands the technique of pre-kissing freshening up. In *The Art of Kissing* (St. Martin's Press, 1991) I described more than twenty-five different types of kisses and kissing techniques, and I've discovered a few more since then, such as lip-o-suction and the butterfly kiss, which are treated in this chapter. These quotes about specific types of kisses and kissing techniques can serve as a kissing reference guide and hopefully will inspire some new kisses for your own experimentation.

♥

BITING KISSES

I leant forward and kissed the blood on her open lips. It sent a zinging through all my limbs and the thirst leapt out for her . . . I drove my teeth into her, feeling her stiffen and gasp, and I felt my mouth grow wide to catch the hot flood when it came.

ANNE RICE, *THE VAMPIRE LESTAT*

BLOWING KISSES

And if you'll blow to me a kiss,
I'll blow a kiss to you.

HORACE AND JAMES SMITH, *THE BABY'S DEBUT* (1812) (THE POEM WAS A PARODY
OF WORDSWORTH)

BUTTERFLY KISSES

She seemed to melt against him in her terror, and he caught her in his arms, held her fast there, felt her lashes beat his cheek like netted butterflies.

EDITH WHARTON, *ETHAN FROME*

COUNTING KISSES

Give me a kiss, add to that kiss a score;
Then to that twenty, add a hundred more:
A thousand to that hundred: so kiss on,
To make that thousand up a million.
Treble that million, and when that is done,
Let's kiss afresh, as when we first begun.

ROBERT HERRICK (1591–1674), *TO ANTHEA: AH, MY ANTHEA!*

❤

Give me a thousand kisses, then a hundred,
Then another thousand, then a second hundred,
Then yet another thousand, then a hundred.
(*Da mi basia mille, deinde centum,*
Dein mille altera, dein secundum centum,
Deinde usque altera mille, deinde centum.)

GAIUS VALERIUS CATULLUS (87–?54B.C.), *CARMINA*, V, 1

She took me to her elfin grot,
    And there she wept, and sigh'd full sore,
And there I shut her wild, wild eyes
    With kisses four.

JOHN KEATS (1795–1821), *LA BELLE DAME SANS MERCI*

ELECTRIC KISSES

A machine to determine electrically the amount of "oomph" in a lady's kiss has recently been built at the University of Richmond. Dr. R. E. Loving, of the Department of Physics, calls the machine an osculometer; students call it "Oscar." To make an "oomph" test, boy and girl each hold an electrode, completing the circuit when they kiss.

ASSOCIATED PRESS (1939)

EYE KISSES

Strephon kissed me in the spring,
  Robin in the fall,
But Colin only looked at me
  And never kissed at all.

Strephon's kiss was lost in jest,
  Robin's lost in play,
But the kiss in Colin's eyes
  Haunts me night and day.

SARA TEASDALE (1884–1933), *THE LOOK*

Ah, let us kiss each other's eyes,
And laugh our love away.

WILLIAM BUTLER YEATS (1865–1939), *LIFE*

THE FRENCH KISS

My parents were married for thirty-one years, and they were hot for each other until my father died. I remember the summer before my father passed away, my mother was in the hospital for something. And on her way into the operating room, my father French kissed her. She smacked him one. My father and mother were so sexy together.

MARILU HENNER, ACTOR ON *EVENING SHADE*

I have a great deal of anger against a church that would teach kids a seven-year-old could burn in hell for French kissing.

ANNE RICE, *CHICAGO TRIBUNE*

Deep Kissing. This is also known as soul kissing, tongue kissing, or French kissing. It may involve tongue-to-tongue contacts, lip and tongue sucking, tongue contacts with the inner surfaces of the lips and with the teeth, deep tongue explorations of the interior of the partner's mouth, contacts with the inner surfaces of the lips of the partner, and the nipping and gentle biting of the tongue and the lips.

ALFRED C. KINSEY ET AL., *SEXUAL BEHAVIOR IN THE HUMAN FEMALE* (1953)

FRIENDLY KISSES

It is quite a delight to receive a well-intentioned and appropriate kiss. Please, feel free to make the gesture.

ELEANOR IRONSIDE, *THE SUNDAY TIMES* (LONDON)

It started as a great romance. Now it's just a friendship with kissing.

HANNAH (JAMIE LEE CURTIS) ON ABC'S *ANYTHING BUT LOVE*

HAND KISSES

Like a storybook Victorian gentleman, gallant and resplendent in his uniform, he kissed her hand. I couldn't believe it. She gave it to him softly, with a trace of embarrassment. And his face hovered down there after the kiss, as if he were staring minutely at her hand.

HOWARD COALE, *THE OUROBOROS*

In diplomatic circles there is a lot of hand kissing . . . I remember a reception in Bucharest in 1972 when a Romanian with a huge red beard bent over to kiss my hand. He was bent over for the longest time and when he finally made it up, there were two long red hairs in my tiger ring.

SHIRLEY TEMPLE BLACK, RETIRED U.S. DIPLOMAT

When a man kisses my hand, I find it neither flattering nor embarrassing and I can only hope he intends a sincere compliment.

ABBEY LINCOLN, SINGER-WRITER

I . . . kiss the tender inward of thy hand.

SHAKESPEARE, SONNET 128

Hand kissing is out of keeping with democratic ideals as a relic of feudal Europe.

PHILIPPA DUKE SCHUYLER, PIANIST-WRITER

I shake a lady's hand—when the lady offers hers first. But a nod and a warm hello is always just as nice. And if I kissed a lady's hand, it would always be with sincerity.

LOUIS ARMSTRONG

The hand kiss is an obstacle to *real* interaction between men and women, and what's more it's discriminatory.

DR. NATHAN HARE, SOCIOLOGIST

One can hardly imagine a young man today being thrilled because he has been permitted to kiss his loved one's hand.

BARBARA CARTLAND, NOVELIST

No rule forbids kissing of a gloved hand . . . Best usage requires that the practitioner not lift up the offered hand toward himself, but incline himself over the hand, lightly brushing it with his lips. It is a mark of respect which one should address only to a married woman. It is rather difficult to execute and is not recommended in the street. In the *salon* [drawing room], it is advisable to reserve the gesture only for the mistress of the house.

DUC DE LÉVIS MIREPOIX, FRENCH HISTORIAN

LEG AND FOOT KISSES

Fain would I kiss my Julia's dainty leg,
Which is as white and hairless as an egg.
ROBERT HERRICK (1591–1674), *ON JULIA'S LEGS*

♥

Anthea bade me kiss her shoe;
I did, and kissed the instep too;
And would have kissed unto her knee,
Had not her blush rebuked me.
ROBERT HERRICK, *HESPERIDES*

LIP-AUGMENTED KISSES

Today movie actors, rock stars, and people who just want to be fashionable are having lip implants. Doctors inject liquid collagen into the lips to make them look plumper and sexier. The temporary treatment lasts only about two months and costs from seven hundred to a thousand dollars. One actor who had the procedure is Barbara Hershey for her role in the 1988 film *Beaches*.

♥

My patients say there's no problem [with lip implants]. No change in the sensation. Kisses are just like they were before, only bigger.

DR. LAWRENCE KOPLIN, PLASTIC SURGEON

♥

They equate the look with sexiness. Young models and actresses come in the day before a photo shoot because they feel fuller lips help create their most appealing look.

DR. RAJ KANODIA, COSMETIC SURGEON WHO PERFORMS UP TO FIFTEEN LIP

AUGMENTATIONS EACH WEEK

LIP-O-SUCTION

When a man kisses the upper lip of a woman, while she in return kisses his lower lip, it is called the "kiss of the upper lip."

THE KAMA SUTRA OF VATSYAYANA (TRANSLATED BY SIR RICHARD BURTON AND

F.F. ARBUTHNOT)

LONG KISSES

Their lips drew near, and clung into a kiss;
A long, long kiss, a kiss of youth and love . . .
Each kiss a heart-quake—for a kiss's strength,
I think, it must be reckon'd by its length.

BYRON (1788—1824), *DON JUAN*

♥

I'll smother thee with kisses . . . Ten kisses short as one, one long as twenty.

SHAKESPEARE, *VENUS AND ADONIS*

♥

Your kiss would mean that I would have to breathe through my nose for its duration.

JACK RICHARDSON, *GALLOWS HUMOR*

O Love, O fire! once he drew
With one long kiss my whole soul thro'
My lips, as sunlight drinketh dew.

TENNYSON (1809–1892), *FATIMA*

A soft lip would tempt you to eternity of kissing!

BEN JONSON (1573–1637), *VOLPONE*

A winning kiss she gave,
A long one, with a free and yielding lip.

WILLIAM BROWNE (C.1591–1643), *BRITANNIA'S PASTORALS*

A kiss,
Long as my exile, sweet as my revenge.

SHAKESPEARE, *CORIOLANUS*

The slowest kiss makes too much haste.

THOMAS MIDDLETON, *A CHASTE MAID IN CHEAPSIDE*

LOOKING WHILE KISSING

Only 8 percent of people keep their eyes open when they kiss.

1992 GALLUP POLL

MAKEUP KISSES

Men hate red lips. They don't like to kiss a woman and have marmalade on their mouths.

PABLO MANZONI, NEW YORK MAKEUP ARTIST

Kisses should not be inspected by those who receive them. Neither should kiss marks: those are the responsibility of the markers, who should exclaim, "Oh, dear, I've left lipstick on you," and offer a clean handkerchief or tissue.

JUDITH MARTIN (MISS MANNERS)

Women don't know anything about a man's perception of a woman wearing lipstick. We ran our own survey among men. It's the first thing they think is sensual about a woman. Second, I found out that the glossy look of lips that is supposed to be so sexy—a lot of men reject that look. They don't want to kiss those lips. They know it's going to be messy and gluey.

SERGIO KAPUSTIN, OWNER OF SERGIO'S EXCLUSIVA, A LIP MAKEUP STUDIO IN

WEST HOLLYWOOD

Seeing an advertisement for an indelible, kiss-proof lipstick reminded me what a wonderful thing it would be if its claims were true . . . I am depressed almost to tears at the thought of the billions and trillions of kisses that never happened because of that confounded red paste that women have been taught to smear upon their lips in the wackiest paradox of modern times. Women make their lips alluring with the very substance that makes it practically impossible to succumb to that allure.

PAUL GALLICO

Mustache Kisses

I shaved my mustache . . . and . . . I now have to learn the subtleties of kissing. Seems my wife complains she feels she is bussing a new man. I think she may be right.

LAWRENCE SHULRUFF, A CHICAGO ATTORNEY

❤

My wife hasn't kissed me much since I stopped shaving.

WILLIAM REBOLINI, HUNTINGTON COUNCILMAN, ON GROWING A MUSTACHE

❤

Being kissed by a man who didn't wax his mustache was—like eating an egg without salt.

RUDYARD KIPLING (1865–1936)

❤

If you men want to know what it's like [to kiss a man with a mustache], take a toothbrush, wet it, and shove it up your nose . . . Add a little salt.

ANITA WISE, COMIC FROM NEW YORK CITY

❤

Mustachios add *quelque chose* [something] to a kiss.

BARBARA COUPER, ACTOR

The Peck

You get into the habit of just pecking your husband. Whatever happened to good, old-fashioned kissing?

ANONYMOUS, *LOS ANGELES TIMES*

SOCIAL KISSES (OR AIR KISSES)

There must be a woman somewhere who hasn't, at one time or another, felt like a clod and an absolute fool while greeting someone. The hand she starts to put out is deflected by the other woman leaning over to kissy-kiss. Or with an air kiss obviously on the way, she offers one cheek and withdraws—too soon, because the other pair of lips is poised for the second cheek. It's a mess.

ENID NEMY, *CHICAGO TRIBUNE*

I'm not wild about them [air kisses]. It's a practice that doesn't seem terribly sincere.

EMILY POST

There is only one proper way to do it. Hold each other's right hand by the fingers. Twist your mouth as far to the left as possible and touch each other lightly on the right side of the jaw. That's the kiss that counts. Anything else is too personal.

JOHN DUKA, *NEW YORK TIMES* FASHION COLUMNIST

Social kissing is more a northern, sophisticated fad that seems to be moving south.

JOANNA HANES, ATLANTA PUBLIC RELATIONS WOMAN

I find myself kissing and wishing I hadn't. You risk being rude if you kiss one person and not another. And there are awkward moments when you don't know whether to kiss or not to kiss. Usually, you kiss just to be safe.

BETSY BLOOMINGDALE, LOS ANGELES SOCIAL LEADER

Increased kissing is part of the general inflation of intimate signals. We kiss people we used to hug, hug people we used to shake hands with, and shake hands with people we used to nod to. Isolated individualism is out. Today separations are not allowed. Everyone is expected to kiss everyone else.

MURRAY DAVIS, SOCIOLOGIST AT THE UNIVERSITY OF CALIFORNIA

Social kissing is often confused with the romantic practice to which it bears a superficial resemblance. This is ridiculous. Does hand-shaking have the same emotional content as holding hands?

JUDITH MARTIN (MISS MANNERS)

In Los Angeles they kiss everyone, whether they know the person or not. In Washington [D.C.] it happens, too. But we would advise you not to kiss everyone. I just don't think it's proper. Kissing should be between very, very close friends, not mere acquaintances, and certainly not strangers. We frown on it, yes.

VIRGINIA DEPEW, *GREEN BOOK* SOCIAL REGISTRY EDITOR

Cheek kissing is a greeting for best friends as well as for hostesses you never met before. Bogart and Wayne and all those big macho guys did it. There was nothing sissy about it.

JAMES BACON, HOLLYWOOD COLUMNIST

TEASING KISSES

She's a big flirt. When you lean in to kiss her, at first she pulls away. But then she come in even closer.

ANONYMOUS PUBLISHER TALKING ABOUT ANNA WINTOUR, *VOGUE'S* EDITOR-IN-CHIEF

TOBACCO KISSES

I thought, "What did I miss about him?" It was the taste of tobacco when I kissed him.

THELMA NORRIS, *CHICAGO TRIBUNE*

Kiss me, I don't smoke.

AMERICAN CANCER SOCIETY STICKER

Q: How do you French kiss a boy who smokes?
A: Quickly.

BRITISH HEALTH EDUCATION AUTHORITY ADVERTISEMENT

May never lady press his lips, his proffer'd love returning,
Who makes a furnace of his mouth, and keeps his chimney
burning;
May each true woman shun his sight, for fear his fumes should
choke her,
And none but those who smoke themselves have kisses for a
smoker.

ANONYMOUS

TWO-CHEEK KISSES (OR CONTINENTAL KISSES)

Hugs, in fact, are becoming increasingly popular and two-cheek kisses are apparently on the wane—or, according to a number of women, should be.

ENID NEMY, *CHICAGO TRIBUNE*

I'm tired of kissing on two cheeks. I hug some people—hugs haven't been as trivialized as kissing.

DENA KAYE, WRITER

♥

Women like to be kissed on both cheeks. They know they're getting a French kiss without all the trouble that usually goes with it.

ART BUCHWALD

♥

Double-cheek kissers have that inexplicable vanity that suffuses some Americans when they believe they are behaving like Europeans.

JUDITH MARTIN (MISS MANNERS)

♥

The goal is not to get a certain number of cheeks kissed. If the cheeks are in any way juxtaposed and the sound of kissing is heard, the ritual has been successfully performed.

JUDITH MARTIN

THE WANDERING KISS

His mouth wandered, wandered, almost touched her ear. She felt the first deep flame run over her . . . He had found the soft down that lay back beyond her cheeks, near the roots of her ears. And his mouth stirred it delicately, as infernal angels stir the fires with glass rods, or a dog on the scent stirs the grass till the game starts from cover.

D.H. LAWRENCE, *MR. NOON* (1934)

♥

INDEX

If you would like to be on the mailing list to receive questionnaires about my upcoming book on romance, please send a self-addressed, stamped, business-size envelope to the address below. (If replying from a foreign country, please include one or more international reply coupons.) *Thank you!*

WILLIAM CANE
P.O. Box 1422
Brookline, MA 02146-0011

The Art of Kissing is a comprehensive guide to making every kiss as tender, fun, passionate, thrilling, and unforgettable as your very first.

As every kissing connoisseur knows, there's more to great kissing than just puckering up. In *The Art of Kissing* lovers will find all the insights they need to add tenderness and technical know-how to all their kisses, from quick, teasing pecks to complicated continental kisses of the highest quality. The book is filled with practical, lips-on advice including do's and don'ts, kissing facts, and loose-lipped personal anecdotes from the first nationwide kissing survey. Also included is a unique "kissing encyclopedia" which lists and details the techniques for more than twenty-five kinds of kisses, including the vacuum kiss, the biting kiss, the electric kiss, the gangster kiss, and the Trobriand Island kiss. You'll even find advice and safety tips for kissing in movie theaters and cars.

At your local bookstore or use this page for ordering. Send it to: Publishers Book & Audio, P.O. Box 120159, Staten Island, NY 10312.

Please send me _____copies of *The Art of Kissing*. I enclose $_____. ($6.95 per copy. Please add $2.50 per order to cover shipping and handling.) Send check or money order payable to St. Martin's Press—no cash or C.O.D.s please.

Name (Please print):_____

Address:_____

City/State:_____ Zip_____

Prices and availability subject to change without notice. Please allow four to six weeks for delivery.